LESSONS FROM EUROPE
A Comparison of British and West European Schooling

Lessons from Europe

A Comparison of British and West European Schooling

MAX WILKINSON

Centre for Policy Studies
London 1977

Centre for Policy Studies
London 1977

First published 1977
by Centre for Policy Studies
Wilfred Street
London SW1.
Photograph by Nick Rogers
Typeset and Printed by
Leighton & Lonsdale Limited
Glenthorne Road, London W6
Ⓒ Centre for Policy Studies
ISBN 0 905880 02 1

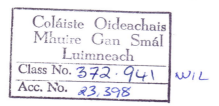

This paper is intended to be an authoritative contribution to the
debate on current economic, social and political issues. The Centre
for Policy Studies does not seek to express a corporate view through
its publications, the authors of which are chosen for their independence
and intellectual vigour.

Contents

Foreword

by Dr. Rhodes Boyson MP

Those of us who taught from the early 1950s to the mid 1970s saw education swept away on a tide of fashion. Innovators, politicians and the trainers of teachers confused change with progress and classroom teachers who complained about what was happening in our schools were classified as reactionary dullards.

Yet fashion is no basis for permanent change and intellectual hemlines can go up as well as down. The year 1976 saw the beginnings of a positive reaction and William Tyndale School, the Bennett Report and the Tameside counter revolution are probably assured of a place in our educational history text books.

Ten years ago progressive euphoria in our schools was at its height. Those of us who wrote in the warning Black Papers were attacked and grossly misrepresented. Now many who led the decline in educational structure and methods are mouthing the words of the Black Papers. Are they to be trusted? Is their conversion genuine or are they simply trying to save their educational and political reputations by climbing on an alternative bandwagon.

Into this new debate comes Max Wilkinson's book. Max Wilkinson was one of the new generation of educational journalists who, in the daily papers, won the respect of many readers. They spend much time in education and in schools and, thus, are not easily hookwinked. They compare notes on methods and approaches.

To improve something it is often important to look at it from outside. Thus Max Wilkinson studies and displays for us educational methods in France, Germany, Holland, Sweden and elsewhere. These are countries which seem to have been economically more successful than has Britain. It seems that we have much to learn from them especially about the degree of central control and the maintenance of a more conservative attitude to change.

The chapters deal with all our present debate. The importance of competition and hard work, the emphasis on language teaching and a broad curriculum, the need for some form of central control, greater vocational and technical emphasis, genuine involvement of parents, the need for more highly qualified and better trained teachers with possibly separate training and qualifications for primary and secondary school service.

There is little doubt that increased expenditure on education and lowered pupil-teacher ratios have not brought the improvement expected throughout our school system. New methods are now suspected and comprehensive reorganisation in many areas is under a cloud.

We thus need a genuine debate and investigation into education. Such a debate will be pointless if it only arises from the very same educational writers, officers and teacher union voices which ten years ago shouted for change and now shout for stability. The pendulum cannot just be swung rapidly backwards and forwards. It is important that any future alterations we make in education are clearly thought out, discussed, introduced on a small scale and all results monitored and published for all to see.

This book raises all the right questions for a genuine debate among parents, teachers, educationalists and politicians. There is a mass of facts and information and by taking its illustrations from Europe-of which we are now part-it is politically neutral in this country. The Centre for Policy Studies has performed a public service by bringing it out and the intelligent and concerned layman as well as the educational specialist will read it with interest and enjoyment.

Rhodes Boyson

I. Introduction

There is one outstanding difference, of which most Britons are unaware, between the ways in which they and all other European countries educate their young.

The countries of Europe have all articulated detailed national policies about what their children shall learn in school and, in many cases, how they shall learn it; in Britain, the major decisions about content and method of education are left to the head teachers and staffs of 27,000 separate schools.

In Sweden, by contrast, the contents and balance of school courses are hotly debated by politicians, industrialists and teachers in a national forum. In France, the studies of each child are under the direct control of the Minister of Education and his regional representatives.

In Britain, however, control and supervision of schools has been delegated to the 125 local education authorities, although the central government does have a number of specific duties. In practice, the Department hardly ever interferes in the running of school courses, while local councillors lack both the time and expertise to take more than a cursory general interest in how head teachers organize the pattern of studies.

The most important consequence has been that the change of methods and style in many, but not all, of our schools has been far more rapid than in most other European countries, although the revolution has been piecemeal and is far from complete.

For this reason, major changes in the character of British schooling have crept into the public consciousness over the last decade with few clear announcements of public policy to precede them and little organized national debate. The transformation of the education system is the result of thousands of individual decisions reflecting the inspirations, the fashions, the idiosyncracies, the political beliefs and the institutional pressures among teachers. The coherence of these changes depends upon the growth of national consensus. It is, therefore, more elusive than the rationale of Continental education

1

which, in theory at least, derives logically from national policy decisions.

In Germany, for example, a comprehensive plan for the reform of the education system, the *Bildungsgesamtplan,* was drawn up and agreed in 1973 by the federal and regional governments. In Sweden, the government is directly responsible for all changes in the system and has, indeed, produced a detailed curriculum for every comprehensive school in the land.

By contrast, the British Labour government's recent Bill on comprehensive schools says nothing about curriculum and very little about organization. The government has confined itself to a brief statement of principle (that children should not be selected for schools by ability) and has left all the details to be worked out by local authorities. It will influence local decisions through circulars, the allocation of money and its power of veto over any plan to change the character of a school, but it will not initiate any coherent national strategy on the form comprehensive education should take.

An important consequence of the British de-centralism is that it is much more difficult than on the Continent to know what is actually going on. Extensive research is required, for example, to find out how many schools are 'progressive' and how many 'traditional', to discover the methods generally used in teaching or the choices of course which children are making. Statistics for the GCE 'O' and 'A' level examinations and for the newer Certificate of Secondary Education for the less able sixteen year-olds give, to be sure, a reasonable idea of the system's output. But, for information on what is happening between the ages of five and sixteen, policy-makers have to rely on a combination of hunch, gossip, sampling and the impressions of the inspectorate.

This is very different from the position in France or Germany, where every year children pass or fail to pass through defined grades of a national curriculum, or in Sweden, where national tests are given regularly to children throughout their careers.

In the 1960s, the British were generally satisfied with their unique method of organized schooling. The freedom given to teachers had allowed the best to flourish unhampered by bureaucratic restraints. The development of new styles of teaching appeared to have enlivened primary schools and to be widening opportunities in the secondary sectors. Meanwhile, standards measured by the university entrance and the examination boards appeared to be rising. The well-publicized successes of the best progressive teachers and the new comprehensive schools led to a general belief that a great leap forward was imminent.

That leap forward has not happened. Indeed, it is now frequently stated that standards are actually falling. A mood of disillusionment and bitterness has replaced the buoyancy of a few years ago. The middle classes who in the late 1950s and 1960s were gradually moving their children away from fee-paying schools, are now returning to them in spite of steep increases in fees. The number of sixth-formers qualifying for university has been considerably lower than expected. The public has been shocked by evidence of a falling standard of basic literacy; the complaints of industrialists have now reached a new stridency.

The crisis of confidence in our education system has arisen when, for the first time since 1945, the average standard of living is falling and the British are slowly awakening to the fact that they are among the poorer countries in Europe.

It is natural, therefore, to look overseas and ask what social and economic qualities have enabled the Germans, Swedes, French and Dutch to develop faster than and, in many respects, overtake the British altogether. It is obvious that, in the long run, the education system must have a major effect on a country's prosperity and well-being. Until recently, most British educationalists have been reluctant to draw any lessons from Europe. Indeed, the traffic has been very much the other way, with experts coming to Britain to study new methods, particularly in primary schools. German schooling has been regarded as too inflexibly traditional, the French as too elitist and centralized and the Dutch system as too peculiar to their religious divisions and trading needs. Only the Swedes, with their comprehensive school system and their search for equality in higher education have provided a popular model for us. However, in some important respects, the Swedish experiment has been misunderstood.

The aim of this study is to compare the developments and aspirations of British education with what has been happening in our nearest neighbours: France, Germany, Holland and Sweden. The method will be, as far as possible, practical with the aim of discussing the qualities and accomplishments necessary to industrial societies if they are to survive and prosper. This approach will immediately raise objections: even to suggest that education is an industrial investment and that pupils are future manpower is to invite protest from the British educational establishment.

For many teachers see, as their main responsibility, the encouragement of individual capacities for personal, academic and imaginative development rather than promoting what they regard as narrow mechanistic skills. Some teachers despise an industrial, materialistic society and conceive their task not as servicing industry's needs but as educating pupils who will change them. This is, perhaps, an extreme statement of the tension between personal, liberal education and the demands of vocational preparation, yet the rapid extension of secondary education and the introduction of comprehensive schooling have brought a new urgency to this issue, although there is little evidence that it is being tackled effectively in Britain.

All West European industrial states are facing a similar problem. The Swedes have, perhaps, been the first to realize the full implications, while the British are the least conscious of it. As Dr Charles Bosanquet said a few years ago when he retired as Vice-Chancellor of Newcastle University: 'We are in danger of producing too many talented consumers and too few producers of wealth'. Many recent trends give

3

added point to his fears and, before considering the position in other European countries, it is as well to look at the grounds for concern in Britain.

First must come the increasing compaints by industrialists of low basic standards of reading, writing and arithmetic. Sir Arnold Weinstock, Managing Director of the General Electric Company reported (1976):

Last year, in more than one of our major industrial cities, the engineering employees failed to recruit as many apprentices as they wanted because not enough school leavers achieved adequate standards. This is a remarkable indictment of our education system and one which raises disturbing questions. The applicants were there; the IQs were there (the tests prove it). But the basic learned skills of literacy and numeracy were not.
What has gone wrong?

Sir Arnold, strongly criticized teachers for helping to perpetuate unhelpful attitudes towards productive industry and said:

Educationists in the schools and the teacher training colleges should recognize that they do no service to our children if they prepare them for life in a society which does not exist and which economic reality will never allow to come into existence unless at a terrible price of freedom and liberty of choice. *(Times Educational Supplement,* 23 January, 1976)

Sir Arnold's views have wide support in industry. Mr Michael Bury, Director of Education and Training for the Confederation of British Industry, told a conference on training in December 1975:

The question of the relationship between the schools and employment has led to a great deal of comment from CBI members. They plainly have continuing and serious misgivings about the standards of achievement of many secondary school leavers, particularly the sixteen year-olds. Much of the comment we have received can only be described as reflecting a genuine anger not, this time, in terms of the difficulties caused for employers, as on behalf of the young people themselves. The view has been expressed that many of these young people, after one of the longest periods of compulsory education in the world, are leaving school in particularly difficult circumstances, badly handicapped for most forms of employment by their lack of elementary skills in reading, writing, arithmetic and communication.

The Electrical Industries Training Board reported at the same conference that many employers were having to send their apprentices back to college — not for further training, but to re-learn the basic mathematics they failed to master at school.

Mr Bury commented:

To seek a solution only after the school leaving age by passing remedial function to employers and further education is neither sensible nor appropriate.

The first evidence of lowered reading standards was provided by the survey in 1970 of the National Foundation for Educational Research which concluded that, after a steady rise since the war, standards had fallen after 1968. The subsequent enquiry, under Sir Alan (now Lord)

4

Bullock, concluded that the general level of competence was well below the requirements of society and that improvement was needed.

(A Language for Life, HMSO, 1975*)*

At the same time, a survey by the Schools Council (What's Going on in Primary Maths?, 1974) showed that a third of teachers believed that the basic processes were being neglected.

The system is also under attack at higher levels for failing to produce enough able and qualified youngsters, particularly in science and technology, who want to go into industry. As a result, some of the science and engineering faculties in universities and polytechnics are now half empty or filled with foreign students and nearly all have empty places.

Lord Bowden, former Principal of the University of Manchester Institute of Science and Technology, said in his annual report for 1974/5:

UMIST has welcomed foreign students for hundreds of years... but we were dismayed when we discovered that there are so few Englishmen in our postgraduate courses that they are dominated by foreign students. In the last four or five years, the composition of some classes has changed dramatically. We have a superb course in machine tool design. For twenty years it was full of Englishmen, scores of whom were sent here by the trade and went back full of new found skill. This year we have eighteen students altogether, only four of whom are British. The trade cannot find any Englishmen to accept the scholarships it has been offering for so long. Our work on the transmission of electric power has traditionally had great influence both here and abroad. This year we have twenty-six students in our MSc class, of whom only one is British. A course in hydrocarbon chemistry, which should be important to the oil industry, has attracted forty-six students, of whom *two* are British-born.

The number of first degree graduates in pure and applied sciences is still declining — their proportion is, at present, only one sixth of the total. In the last few years, the Standing Conference of University and Polytechnic Appointments Officers has reported a reluctance by graduates to opt for posts in industry. The proportion of first degree graduates going into industry was only 18.4 per cent in 1973/74, in spite of high demand from firms. In 1975, in spite of the severe recession, industry was offering more jobs to graduates than they were prepared to take. These recent trends must be seen in the light of the broad general prejudice against industry which flourished in universities for many years. Research, the civil service and the professions have, traditionally, had greater prestige and, in many ways, have offered better rewards to graduates. As a result, Britain has suffered a steady drain of much of the best talent away from productive industry. This tendency is in sharp contrast to Japan, where service with a good industrial company brings very high prestige. In Germany and France also, the prestige of engineers has traditionally been much higher than in Britain and it is worth noting that, in Germany and Sweden, the engineering faculties at universities are over-subscribed.

It would seem obvious that training of large numbers of highly qualified engineers ought to be a priority in a trading nation like Britain, particularly at a time when many traditional industries are losing their competitiveness, yet there is evidence that the study of science and mathematics in our secondary schools is at a very low ebb.

As long ago as 1968, the report by Sir Frederick Dainton (Cmnd 3541) on science education drew attention to the downward spiral by which a shortage of good science teachers produces a shortage of good sixth-formers in the subject, which in turn results in a shortage of scientists among the next generation of teachers. Since the Dainton report, the new styles of science courses developed by the Nuffield Foundation have spread widely in schools. A new type of mathematics, intended to be broader, more attractive and less difficult has been developed by the Schools Mathematics Project and is now used in about a fifth of secondary schools. In addition, a new type of combined science degree has been developed by several universities with the intention of providing less specialized studies in the subject.

In spite of all these efforts, there has been very little improvement: the proportion of GCE 'A' Level entries in science is still declining. In 1950, 54 per cent of all 'A' Level subjects attempted were in science. By 1973, the proportion had fallen to 39 per cent. The proportions of mathematics subjects were: 1955 - 15 per cent and 1973 - 13 per cent.

More worrying, the proportion of teachers who have good science and mathematics qualifications has taken a veritable nose-dive in the last year or two. Government figures *(First Destination of Graduates 1972/73,* HMSO, 1974) show that the number of women graduates going into science teaching fell by nearly half in four years to only sixty. The number of men fell by 45 per cent over two years. In primary schools, the situation is hardly better for, in 1975, over 40 per cent of students accepted for teacher training courses did not even possess a GCE 'O' Level certificate in mathematics. This is particularly disturbing at a time of rapid change of the primary school curriculum, when the new mathematics is introducing quite sophisticated concepts to young children. For it is generally admitted that replacing the old-fashioned chanting of tables and the lists of sums by more flexible teaching puts extra demands on the teacher if it is to be effective.

Professional alarm over the decline in science subjects was expressed forcibly by Mr R. Schofield of the Department of Education, Brunel University, in the *Physics Bulletin* May 1975. After discussing the difficulties of teaching the subject in mixed ability comprehensive schools, he said:

Calls are voiced for the need to devise a form of physics curriculum with, at the most, minimal mathematics content. It would not be reasonable to argue that such a subject would not be worth learning but is would be proper to point out that it is unlikely to be suitable for someone proposing to enter physics or engineering as a vocation. In the absence of reliable data, no one is able to comment with authority but I believe we are most likely to find that

6

a lowering of standards has taken place.

For these reasons, I regard it as entirely likely that general standards of physics attainment in schools will drop and the subject even disappear from the curriculum. It is possible that 'honours standard' physics would only be undertaken in the postgraduate schools of relatively few universities.

Some educationists, particularly non-scientists, regard the plight of science with unconcern. This is partly because of the peculiar British snobbery between different subjects resulting from the early specialization required by GCE 'A' Level. The decline of science is regarded with suppressed glee by some quite intelligent people. One former professor of education asked me: 'What is the use of science — does it make you a more effective *operator?*'. Others, more rational, blame the dry conservatism of physics syllabuses which, until recently, were heavily dependent on the rote learning of facts and formal proofs discovered in the nineteenth century.

Now, there are unhappy signs that language teaching, a vital area for a commercial nation, is beginning the same downward spiral as the sciences. A ten-year experiment in the teaching of oral French in primary schools has virtually collapsed.

In her report on the project (National Foundation for Educational Research, 1974) Dr Clare Burstall concluded that primary school French lessons did little to encourage further study of the language and, in a considerable proportion of cases, it had a negative effect by putting children off the subject. And the failure of the primary schools experiment is the least important.

The number of pupils passing GCE 'A' Level French each year has fallen by 1,400 between 1966 and 1973, at a time when overall passes increased by 20 per cent. Passes in German are also static and the proportion of all passes in a modern language is only 6.9 per cent.

At 'O' Level, the number of pupils passing in French, fell by 9,000, or about 10 per cent, between 1963 and 1973. *(School Leavers CSE and GCE, 1973,* HMSO, 1975)

As a result, university and polytechnic language departments are, for the first time since the war, having difficulty in recruiting enough suitable students.

When faced with these trends, it is difficult to resist the view that the unique degree of freedom allowed in the British decentralized system has tended to promote, among teachers and pupils alike, a drift away from the 'difficult' subjects. These are the disciplines and the painful mastery of skills and techniques needed before the higher intellectual or imaginitive abilities can take flight. Mathematics and languages, like piano playing, demand long, hard practice before the rewards are tasted. (The playing of musical instruments is also on the decline). By contrast, English and History have always offered more obvious gratification at an elementary level, providing earlier chances for the pupil to 'take-off' into speculation or analysis of his own. The recent trend has been for the development of a whole range of hybrid subjects under such banners as 'integrated courses' or 'environmental studies'. They attempt to combine gratification, often termed 'relevance', with elements of the traditional disciplines culled from formerly different subjects. The inherent danger of this approach is that the mastery of specific skills will either be sacrificed intentionally or, more likely, just lost in the fog.

This raises the central question of how to achieve the right balance of skills, factual knowledge, imaginative endeavour and character training. It is an issue which provokes very great disagreement in Britain and on which there are important differences in Europe which will be discussed more fully in a later chapter.

However, before considering what lessons can be learnt from other countries, we should pause to look at two other criticisms of our own schooling which have recently been gaining force and which are both related. The first is that schools are failing to prepare pupils for their future jobs and the second is that they are not giving enough attention to the preparation for future citizenship, that important function which in Communist countries is called ideological training and, in religious communities, moral guidance.

The gulf between schooling and future employment was brought to public attention by the Government's inspectors (HMIs) in a report on schools' careers advice *(Careers Education in Secondary Schools,* October, 1973). The reports, from 150 inspectors and a survey of 870 schools, showed only tenuous links with industry. Careers advice to children was inadequate, mainly because schools gave a low priority to this aspect of their work. Careers teachers were often deprived of such elementary requirements as filing cabinets and telephones.

More seriously, the report showed that schools were making little or no effort to plan their courses with childrens' future careers in mind. Only 8 per cent of schools had an 'established and profitable' relationship with local industry and some schools quite simply did not understand the need to help pupils towards future jobs.

This failure by many schools to come to terms with the world of work and its demands may, in some cases, have deep roots in the philosophy of education and social traditions which have developed over the years. A chance remark made by one comprehensive school headmaster illustrates the point. It was made at the rehearsal for an Inner London Education Authority closed circuit television discussion on the effects of raising the school leaving age to 16. As a preliminary to the discussion, the authority recorded a short documentary film of school activities: this showed some 16 year-olds busily engaged in metalwork, while the commentator explained that they were being given a foretaste of the kind of work they would be doing after school.

The headmaster, who is among the city's most respected and influential, demanded, with some passion, that the commentary should be changed: he said that the whole purpose of the modern comprehensive school was to give pupils higher ambitions than this kind of 'routine' industrial work.

8

'But who is going to do these necessary and important jobs, if your pupils will not?' he was asked. His answer was that industry must be changed so that these dull jobs would be mechanized out of existence.

This brief exchange illustrates a thorough confusion in many schools between the admirable aim of encouraging individual pupils to extend themselves and climb the academic ladder and, on the other hand, the need to be realistic about the jobs which the majority of children are *likely* to fill and, indeed, *must* fill if Britain is to produce the wealth on which education depends.

At some stage in their education, nearly everyone must move from the goals of liberal academic education to the acquisition of specific, often narrower vocational aptitudes. (Teachers have been among the few groups exempted from this rule). It is obvious that a child destined for a manual or semi-skilled job will make the switch earlier than one who is going to be a technical expert or an administrator. But, at what stage, should the changeover take place and what should be its form? Should comprehensive schools provide workshop and other specific training to more pupils and at an earlier age?

Would the less able children be happier and more disciplined in secondary schools if they were spending more time learning the skills which they could believe to be useful? Is learning to be a skilled lathe operator, for example, inherently less valuable or less dignified than learning, say, geography?

The British answer to these questions is a result of drift rather than of any careful strategy. This drift has taken us further away from vocational objectives than other European countries, notably Holland; while in Sweden, the effects of comprehensive schooling and a drive towards equality on vocational training have been considered much more carefully than in Britain.

There are several other reasons for believing that a reappraisal of the balance of our education is now overdue. They can be summarized as:
1. Employers' complaints are broadening from the lack of basic skills to unsatisfactory attitudes towards work which, it is believed, schools are helping to foster.
2. Growing indiscipline reported by all the teachers' unions and, indeed, the subject of a Government enquiry. Social factors outside the control of schools are, clearly, a major cause but there is little doubt that bad behaviour and vandalism are also symptoms of a dissatisfaction by pupils with what the schools are providing. Pupils who feel they are getting somewhere are much less likely to break up lessons, smash windows or resort to arson. Yet these behaviour patterns are increasing.
3. Further evidence of pupils' and parents' alienation from the aims of schools was provided in an important survey by the Schools Council (Enquiry I, 1968) which revealed a fundamental cleavage of aspirations. Parents wanted their children to learn basic and recognisable skills like literacy and mathematics and to be prepared by their teachers for earning a living. Pupils generally agreed and put a surprisingly high value on the 'hard' subjects, like mathematics.

Teachers, on the other hand, put much greater emphasis on the liberal educational goals of developing creative, personal and moral qualities.

There are, however, several powerful obstacles to any concerted change in Britain and, particularly, to a change in the direction of more vocational emphasis. These are, briefly:

1. The background and training of school-teachers who generally have little experience outside the school and college system, in spite of some attempts by industry and commerce to arrange visits for them.

2. The current preoccupation with equality, especially in the developing comprehensive schools. This makes it difficult for teachers to steer children too decisively away from the main academic streams, for fear of re-introducing the irreversible selection which was such an unpopular aspect of the old eleven-plus exam.

3. Inadequate equipment and staffing of technical and workshop departments in many comprehensive schools. Vocational education is more expensive than most 'liberal' education.

4. Traditional prejudice in favour of 'academic' courses. The academic route with university or college as destination and GCEs as milestones has, in the past, carried the highest social status. It has been the highway to the professions and the escape route for bright working class children from the mines, the docks, the railways and other jobs which, until recently, offered low status and low pay.

5. As a result of this general prejudice, the new development of courses in secondary schools has tended to repeat the old academic pattern. Thus, the rapidly expanding Certificate of Secondary Education offers courses which largely mirror, at a lower level, those provided for the top 30 to 40 per cent in the GCE 'O' Levels. Efforts have been made to make academic subjects more 'relevant' to the experience of lower ability pupils (for example, by focusing combined history and geography on local institutions and 'our town' or by use of the project method). However, the old academic aims of broadening the pupils' intellects and providing a general grasp of facts have not generally been re-examined. This is partly because teachers have seen the ideal of 'secondary education for all' as a chance to free children from the narrow Victorian concept of moulding each youngster for a future station in life. Consequently, teachers have, on the whole, failed to reconsider whether the aims of personal development and equal opportunity could be achieved equally well within a school programme geared more specifically to the world of work. This point will be considered in more detail in the context of differing solutions in Europe.

6. A further obstacle to change in the British system is the sharp division between the schools and the further education provided in the technical colleges. The colleges, covered by different rules, different staffing standards and different conditions of service, have traditionally provided the specific vocational education demanded by industry. As a result, such courses have tended to be excluded from schools, so that a youngster wanting to take a course leading, for example, to the building

or engineering trades, must necessarily wait until he (or she) has passed the school-leaving age of 16. This, in itself, may be undesirable, particularly now that the leaving age has been raised. But there is also a built-in incentive for schools to try to retain pupils after the school-leaving age when they would be better off in a technical college. Salaries of school staff, for example, as well as the public esteem of a school, depend partly on the size of its sixth form. Even teachers who are entirely disinterested, as no doubt many are, have a further motive for trying to maintain a large sixth form: more pupils will result in more expert staff being available to improve the teaching of all age groups. In addition, teachers have an understandable desire to inspire loyalty and affection for their school which, where successful, will inevitably encourage youngsters to stay on for an extra year. As a result of these pressures, teachers are now campaigning for the introduction of a new examination to be called the Certificate of Extended Education (CEE) which will, effectively, extend the lower standard of education provided by the CSE course up to the age of 17.

The effect of this examination would be to further institutionalize the type of general education currently offered in our schools and to pre-empt the demands for a greater emphasis on the vocational skills which are largely taught in the colleges.

At the same time, colleges are, for a variety of reasons, moving more and more into the field of general education and providing an increasing number of GCE 'O' and 'A' Level courses. The division between the schools and technical colleges is, therefore, appearing to be more and more arbitrary, and several influential figures led by Lord Alexander, former secretary of the Association of Education Committees, have proposed a more integrated scheme for the education and training of 16 to 19 year-olds.

It is important to consider whether the arbitrary dividing line between our colleges and schools is really justified by anything more than tradition. A comparison with the Swedish system, which is totally integrated, and the Dutch system, which has been fragmented into hundreds of different trade and vocational schools, will also illuminate the sector in Britain.

In the end, however, the details of the curriculum and of organization are less important than the attitudes and values which teachers communicate to their pupils. This was recognized historically by the religious foundations which established many of our voluntary schools and it has been the informing principle of many of the great public schools which still couple 'Godliness and good learning' as inseparable aims and lay tremendous stress on methods of character formation.

Recently, however, many of the traditional methods of character training schools have been falling into disuse or, at least, assuming a much less important place. This is partly the result of society's trend towards permissiveness and a questioning of authority, partly because of the development of bigger schools and partly because liberal teachers have stressed personal and intellectual scepticism at the expense of corporate discipline. Thus, organized games, the prefect system, school rules and discipline, uniforms and communal worship are all less highly regarded than they were fifteen years ago. In some comprehensive schools, for example, competitive team games have all but disappeared: in other schools, the minimum provision of the 1944 Education Act for a daily act of worship and regular instruction in religion is evaded or ignored. Intellectual liberalism has, indeed, gone so far that Church interests were able to agree a religious syllabus in Birmingham which includes a section on Communism along with other 'stances for living'.

Individually, these changes may not be of very great significance; after all, there are plenty of arguments for liberalizing discipline and for bringing religious instruction more in line with modern practice. But, cumulatively, the changes, particularly in discipline and 'school spirit', may be affecting a profound shift of attitudes to society and work amongst the present generation of children. This shift, for which television must bear a major responsibility, can be seen in all industrial countries. But the current fashion for minimizing the influence of schooling has gone too far. In Germany and France, disciplined schooling has almost certainly had an effect on teenagers' eventual attitudes to work.

In an age of doubt and cynicism, it is, perhaps, expecting too much of teachers to give children firm, moral values. Teachers, no doubt, represent the full spectrum of moral and religious beliefs, as they do political convictions. (A survey for the Times Educational Supplement by National Opinion Polls before the February 1974 election, showed that they were about evenly divided between the three parties). Nevertheless, the replacement of old certainties by the principles of freedom and tolerance has allowed into the profession a vociferous minority opposed to our society and even actively wishing to destroy it. These intellectual revolutionaries, mainly clustered around Trotskyite persuasions, have had wide ripples of influence out of proportion to their numbers. They have a considerable minority following within the universities and polytechnics and in a small number of schools, particularly in London, their voice has been dominant. Their reverence for the ideal of the class struggle has led to an attack on scholastic standards (because they provide a ladder for the middle class) and a loathing for vocational courses (because they help the ruling class to exploit the children of the workers). Doubtless, the majority of teachers have no sympathy with the extremists' revolutionary mythology yet many younger teachers find it hard to argue against some of their educational conclusions. For recent research *(Inequality* by Christopher Jenks, 1972, and *Education Priority,* Volume 3, 1975) has clearly shown that children from deprived working class homes suffer a pre-destined disadvantage in a school system which uses traditional measures of achievement. In addition, many teachers are, for reasons already summarised, deeply suspicious of anything which looks like training for jobs.

If the ultra-left have, as yet, little political muscle, the more established Marxists centred on the Communist party, undoubtedly do exert wide influence. The 'militants', led by Communists and Marxist sympathisers have, since 1969, held a powerful, though not always dominant, position within the National Union of Teachers — the largest union. The chairman of their education committee is a Communist and one of their leading thinkers on education matters for the last decade has been Mr Max Morris, who was an executive member of the Communist party. The colleges of education have also had their share of lecturers with beliefs in the hinterland between democratic socialism and communism. They have often formed a loose alliance with those suffering from the least logical mutations of liberalism claiming to be vaguely descended from Rousseau and Dewey.

Union pressure has combined with the writings of distinguished Communist intellectuals like Professor Brian Simon, Director of the Institute of Education at Leicester University and the action research of socialists like Dr A.H. Halsey at Oxford University and Dr Eric Midwinter in Liverpool.

One consequence of this concerted emphasis of the system's obvious shortcomings, has been to undermine the confidence of teachers in their traditional values. Secondly, the left-wing lobby has promoted beliefs about equality and equal opportunity which have inherent contradictions and which, in the hasty tempo of staffroom discussion can be muddled and confused. Thirdly, the preoccupation with equality has led to a belief that everyone is necessarily competing in the same academic race. Dr Midwinter did, to be sure, realize the futility of this thesis but his work in Liverpool primary schools ran up a blind alley by trying to redefine the aims of a traditional liberal education in terms of working class language and culture. *(Education and the Community,* George Allan & Unwin, 1975).

The alternative possibility of giving children an early option to develop practical skills and craft training as an integral part of a more general school course has been frowned on by the left and therefore it has not been adequately explored.

In Holland, this has been accepted for years while in Germany, the highly organized apprenticeship schools have provided a much superior practical training to that offered to the majority of British children. In this context, Swedish upper secondary schools are of particular interest because, while pursuing equality, they have been careful to recognize differences in aptitude by providing a system of highly differentiated courses for the academically less able.

In Britain, the case for a thorough re-think has been strongly reinforced by recent trends in the distribution of incomes. At a time when plumbers can earn as much as hospital doctors and more than teachers, failure or lack of interest in the academic hurdle race is becoming less of a disaster. If the trend continues, it may be possible even for socialists to return to the basic premise of the 1944 Act; to accept that people are different and that their different abilities and aptitudes require different types of education if they are to be fully realized.

Opposition to the eleven-plus has obscured the fact that selection is inevitable at some time or another even if, as in Germany, a large element of free choice is left to the pupil and his parents. If academic standards are maintained, many children will simply drop out or fall behind. This happens in Japan where the curriculum is standard for all children up to the age of 16. The alternatives are to provide watered down academic courses for the less able (which has been the tendency in Britain) to reduce overall standards (which has happened in the USA) or to provide a larger number of different courses (as in Holland).

Now that equality of incomes has been more nearly approached than at any time in our history and when income differentials are amongst the smallest of any of the industrialized nations, it may be time to reconsider whether the Dutch system is not of more interest to us than the American.

II. Education in Europe –
How they do it on the Continent

Before considering some of the details of how our European neighbours organize their education systems, it will be as well to look in broad outline at the different methods of control. As already mentioned, Britain is the only country in which the curriculum is largely delegated to individual schools and the implications of this will be examined in a subsequent chapter.

Administratively, England and Wales are divided into 104 local education authorities, with a further 17 for Scotland and Northern Ireland and four in the Channel Islands, the Isle of Man and the Scillies. The authorities own the maintained schools and have charge of their running, subject to certain general restraints imposed by central government. Detailed supervision is supposed to be undertaken by managers (primary schools) and governors (secondary schools) who are mostly appointed by the authority, although there is, increasingly, provision for the election of teachers, parents and pupils. The powers of the governors and managers are somewhat varied and ill-defined. Nominally they have oversight of the curriculum and the appointment of staff and head-teachers but, in practice, the curriculum is usually left to the head, who also has the effective voice in the appointment of staff (in some authorities, this is not the case). The local authority officials and inspectors (now often called advisers) usually have a strong influence over the appointment of head-teachers.

Here too, in some authorities, the officials are all-powerful; in others, for example County Durham and Wales, the elected councillors of the education committee often determine the choice and, sometimes, as a recent case at Highbury Grove Comprehensive School in North London showed, a powerful body of governors can choose their own head and even over-ride the choice of their authority. Once appointed, heads and staff are very difficult to remove from office because of the lengthy disciplinary proceedings which have been agreed with the unions.

Supervision is exercised by the local authorities' subject inspectors (or advisers) and through Her Majesty's Inspector of Schools (HMIs). The

15

strength of the local inspectors varies considerably. In Inner London, for example, a large inspectorate is maintained so that the HMIs seldom venture into the city's schools. In July 1968, the inspectorate admitted to the Parliamentary Select Committee on Education that regular five year full inspections by HMIs were being phased out. Since then, they have concentrated more on fact-gathering, collating and advising on good practice and directing support towards weak teachers or bad schools. Local inspectors have also taken on a much more advisory role in keeping with the change of name. They visit schools to make suggestions, co-ordinate teachers' efforts and mount courses, rather than to examine.

Local authorities also pay running expenses of the voluntary schools which have independent governors, mainly from religious and charitable foundations. In the past, the voluntary schools have been largely integrated with the maintained sector, although they have tended to have a more formal and more religious tilt to their courses.

The authorities also maintain colleges of education for teacher training, colleges of technology and the new polytechnics. In practice, however, much of the expenditure for higher education is pooled — authorities spread the cost using a central fund to which they all contribute. One consequence of councillors voting expenditure largely raised in other areas, has been slack financial control.

Central control is exercised by the government through the Department of Education and Science, mainly by financial restraints on building programmes and, indirectly, through the rate support grant to local authorities.

In a recent memorandum to the Parliamentary Expenditure Committee (Education, Arts and Home Office Sub-Committee) on 10 November 1975, the Department defined its influence thus:

The Department is essentially a policy-making body — not an executive agency. It does not run any schools or colleges or engage any teachers... or prescribe any text books or curricula. Its policy-making functions extend from defining, from time to time as necessary, specific policies — some large, some small — to establishing a general framework governing the direction, pace and scale of developments in the education service as a whole. Although the Department has no substantial executive functions, policy formation itself involves a good deal of administration and the education status place other duties of a regulatory kind upon it. For example, the Department:
a.   Sets minimum standards of educational provision.
b.   Controls the rate, distribution and cost of educational building.
c.   In consultation with local authority associations, forecasts the level of local authority expenditure on education to be taken into account when determining the size of the rate support grant.
d.   Supports financially, by direct grant, a limited number of institutions of a special kind.
e.   Determines the numbers and balances of teachers in training and decides the principles governing the

recognition of teachers as qualified.

f.   Administers a superannuation scheme for teachers.

g.   Supports educational research through the agency of the National Foundation for Educational Research, university departments and other bodies.

h.   Settles disputes — for example between a parent and a local education authority or between the local education authority and the managers of a school.

France

The French system offers a complete contrast with our own because, as Fig. 1 shows, all responsibility devolves ultimately from the minister. The bureaucracy is divided into ten directorates dealing with the different areas of responsibility, including the curriculum as well as the administration of the various sectors.

The administration is effected through 23 regions, *académies,* each covering a full range of provision from primary schools to universities. The head of each *académie,* or the *rector,* is also chancellor of all the universities in his *académie.* The *rector* thus combines the functions of an academic, a director of local education, a public servant and, as the minister's delegate, something of a politician. The *académies* are, on average, about five times as large as the British local education authorities.

However, in some respects, the staff of the *académies* have less responsibility than British education authorities. The curriculum, for example, is laid down by ministerial decree after consultations with various councils, committees and commissions — including members appointed by the ministry and representatives of various interests, including the teachers' associations. The ministry also lays down the standards of teacher training and has power to allocate teachers to schools anywhere in France. Thus, the regional administrations do not have the same burden of recruiting and placing teachers as do our local authorities.

The state also runs all the major examinations whereas, in Britain, this duty devolves on eight GCE Boards, thirteen CSE Boards controlled by teachers, and eleven further specialist examining boards — a total of thirty-two boards, all independent of state control.

Compulsory schooling begins at six in primary schools with a common curriculum up to the age of 11. It continues to 16 in the new *collèges d'enseignement secondaires* (CES) which are comprehensive institutions combining the old *lycées* (grammar schools) with the *collèges d'enseignement général* (secondary modern). Children are allocated to different streams according to ability on leaving their primary schools. Then, at 16, further selection takes place for various academic and vocational courses ranging from one to three years — some of them in technical colleges.

At 15, some pupils are allowed to leave full-time schooling to take up apprenticeships, provided that they return to school for a year's part-time studies. Those who stay in the *lycée* stream to take the *baccalauréat* generally expect to go to university. Formerly, a

17

18

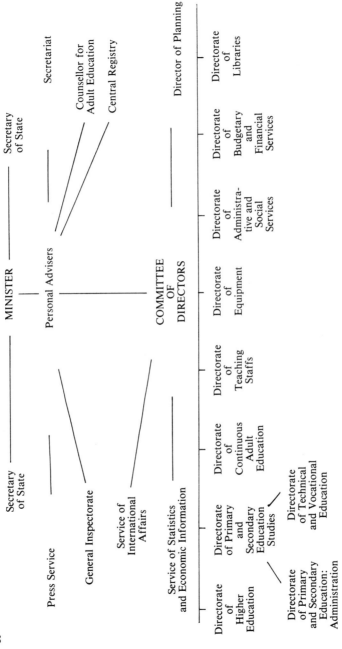

Fig. 1

baccalauréat automatically entitled the student to a university place but, with increasing pressure of student numbers, some faculties are now having to impose *numerus clausus* or restricted competitive entry.

Very considerable changes were proposed by the Education Minister, M. René Haby, following the July 1975 Education Act. The aim is to allow greater flexibility by ensuring that all children study basically the same course up to the age of 16. However, the reforms are also based firmly on the recognition of differences of ability between children. Thus, even at the age of 6, when children enter the primary school, differences in ability will be catered for. After 8 weeks' initial observation, children will be divided into two groups. The cleverer will complete the first cycle in one year whilst the slower learners will take two years on the basic preparatory cycle, mastering the simplest skills. In the later primary level cycles, similar arrangements will be made to set up groups by ability in different subjects.

In secondary schools, all children will, in theory, follow the same basic curriculum but, clearly, children will progress at different speeds so that distinct ability groups will emerge. Differentiation will start at 13 (the second cycle of the lower secondary school) when pupils will be able to choose different options.

For the cleverer children, there will be two types of *lycée* — the academic type as it exists now and a new *lycée* aimed to provide a more vocational content, the *lycée d'enseignement professionnel.* The three year course in the traditional *lycée,* comprises two years of predominantly general studies common to all pupils, followed by a year of specialization. At the professional *lycée,* which replaces the present technical education colleges, students will follow two-year courses leading to the certificate of professional aptitude or the diploma of professional studies. Those who are successful, can go on to a general *lycée* to take the *baccalauréat* and go on to university. The reform thus aims to upgrade the status of technical education and vocational education by marrying it with the high prestige of the traditional *baccalauréat.*

At the same time, efforts are being made to increase the vocational slant of university studies.

Germany

In Germany, the organization of schooling is somewhat between the extremes of French centralism and devolution to localities, as in Britain. Education is run by the eleven separate provincial governments or *Länder.* Policies differ considerably between the *Länder* which are autonomous and determine the curricula for all the schools in their jurisdiction. Compulsory schooling lasts from the age of 6 to 16 (although the last year is optional in some *Länder*). A common primary school takes children up to 10 when they are 'guided', according to performance and their school records into one of three types of education: the academic *Gymnasium,* which leads to the *Abitur* or university entrance exam; the *Realschule,* which prepares children up to the age of 16 for intermediate technical qualification; and the *Hauptschule,* which continues general and vocational education for the least able. In many cases, the *Hauptschuler,* which cater for just under half the children, are continuations of the primary or *Grundschule.*

National policy is co-ordinated by the Permanent Conference of Education Ministers, jointly with the Federal Government, although power is vested in the *Länder.* The existence of separate *Länder* has proved an obstacle to concerted planning at national level, but their rights have been safeguarded by memories of the way Hitler used central control to force propaganda and political ideology on to schools.

In June, 1973, the Government's Federal State Commission produced the first 'Overall Education Plan' intended as a long-term framework for the development of the system up to 1985.

The main burden of this plan was the need for a more uniform system to provide more 'equality of opportunity'. But this concept is interpreted very differently in different *Länder.* The six *Länder* with Christian Democratic (Conservative) governments want to see a slow development of comprehensive institutions in which the three separate types of schooling, corresponding roughly to our grammar, technical and secondary moderns, retain their separate identities. This is similar to the French model. The other *Länder* wish, however, to move towards integrated comprehensive schools more similar to the British model. The initial proposal is for comprehensive schooling only up to the age of 16.

At present, only a few states, notably Hesse, have moved towards fully comprehensive schools (Gesamtschule) on any scale and these are still mainly experimental.

One notable feature of German education is that the great majority of children only go to school in the mornings. The school day starts earlier than in Britain, however, and considerably more homework is set. In spite of the half-day schooling, comparative surveys by the Institute for Educational Evolution in Stockholm indicate that German children reach as good a standard as those in countries with full-time schooling.

Holland

The dichotomy between the need for state control and the pressure for local initiative in education has been solved in a unique way in Holland. Any group of parents or citizens may found a private school which will, automatically, qualify for state subsidy under certain conditions. This is analogous to the British system by which voluntary controlled and aided schools receive all their running costs from public funds. There are, however, two important differences.

The first is that public money is provided directly by the central government rather than, as in Britain, through the elected local authorities. The second difference is that, as a condition for maintaining the schools, the government insists on a fairly tight control of the curriculum through inspections and lays down a series of explicit standards.

Owners of private schools thus have the same relationship with the government as the municipal authorities who own some schools but have to comply with national standards. Holland, thus, has three types of school administration, all closely dovetailed: first, those owned privately — mainly by religious groups — which are state maintained; secondly, those owned by the municipal authorities but subject to general state control; and thirdly, fully state schools.

The constitutional amendment in 1917 which put public and private schools on an equal financial footing has since been extended to other types of school, with the result that the majority of Dutch schools are in private ownership.

Just under a third of primary and general secondary schools are in the public sector, compared with between 40 and 44 per cent owned by the Roman Catholics and between 22 and 27 per cent owned by the Protestants. Overall, 65 per cent of education expenditure goes on private schooling.

The proportion of grammar school and university students in the public sector is, however, higher at 73 per cent. The fully state schools tend, therefore, to have the highest prestige because they prepare pupils for university entrance. By contrast, all primary schools and some of the more general secondary schools are run by the municipal authorities.

The consequence of stressing the importance of private initiative in the founding of schools has been a proliferation of specialized secondary institutions. Parents have a choice of ten different types of secondary education — five of which give general education to different levels while the other five provide lower technical and vocational training for different, often very specific types of job.

Most Dutch children start nursery school at the age of 4 (over 80 per cent) and 95 per cent are in nursery classes by the age of five. Compulsory primary schooling starts at 6, and, traditionally, was regulated by a strict progression of grades regulating standards. At 12 plus, the children take an entrance examination for academic secondary schools or different combinations of test and educational guidance for the more vocational schools.

These secondary schools range from the academic *lyceum* sometimes subdivided into the science-based and the arts-based *gymnasium* and *athaneum* respectively. Non-academic general education is divided into schools of different levels. The highest is the HAVO (higher general secondary school). Next comes MAVO (lower general secondary school). Finally there is a variety of lower technical and vocational schools (LBO).

There are eight main types of school preparing children for different occupations, for example housepainting, fishery, inland navigation or dock working, hairdressing, office work or small-scale trade and enterprise.

The school leaving age is, at present, 16 but proposals recently put out for discussion by the Education Minister, Dr Jos van Kemenade, envisage raising the leaving age to 18 in 1985.

Dr van Kemenade's discussion paper 'The Future Educational Order' (July 1975) seeks much more flexible opportunities than are allowed in the present rather rigid and examination-bound system in which choices at 12 often determine, not merely the level of a child's education, but the precise nature of his future job. The present 12-plus would be abolished and replaced by a comprehensive middle school. Selection would then take place at 16 when children competed for various types of upper school.

Sweden

The Swedish system is believed, by progressive educationalists, to be the most advanced in Europe; and in many respects the belief is true. The Swedes have smaller classes, more children staying on at school voluntarily; educational research is more systematic than elsewhere, the planning of courses to fit future vocations is more explicit and, above all, the move over to a more egalitarian comprehensive system is more established.

The move towards a comprehensive system was started in 1950; it was completed for the compulsory school range (ages 7 to 16) in 1968 and, since then, there has been a further integration in the upper secondary schools, although they are divided into distinct 'lines' for pupils of different aptitudes. The widening of educational opportunity to all who can benefit from it, has also affected universities where a big effort is being made to recruit students from employment, rather than straight from school, and to waive the need for paper qualifications.

Sweden, in common with France, imposes a central curriculum on all schools and the balance of studies has been the subject of lively public debate. Schools are managed by the 280 municipal councils, but the most important aspects of school administration are the responsibility of the National Board of Education which comes under the Ministry.

The basic comprehensive school system covers the whole of the compulsory age range when children of all abilities are taught together for most of the time although, at the age of 13, they are able to choose between different options — the first explicit distinction between the bright and the duller pupils.

After the age of 16, paths diverge. Most pupils go on to the upper secondary school (90 per cent stay at least until they are 18): a third go on to *gymnasium* streams which provide a three year course leading to university. As, however, it is possible to repeat a year at one particular grade, the average age on leaving the *gymnasium* is over 20.

Those who do not go to the *gymnasium* can take a whole range of two-year courses in general, technical and specifically vocational subjects. The *fackskola* (continuation school) offered general vocational courses whilst the *yrkeskola* (vocational school) offered mainly full-time apprenticeships. These schools are now integrated in the upper secondary school which thus encompasses much of the area of the British further education and technical colleges.

22

The integrated upper secondary school provides some 20 different lines of study at different levels with courses lasting two or three years. The courses are now divided by subject area rather than level of difficulty and the range is indicated on the table:

Arts and Social Subjects SO	Economics and Commercial	Technical and Science subjects
2-year lines Consumer Line Consumer and Nursing Line Music Line Nursing Line Social Line	2-year lines Distribution and Clerical Line Economics Line	2-year lines (see list)*
3-year lines Liberal Arts Social Sciences	3-year line Economics Line	3-year line Natural Sciences 4-year line (can be done in 3 years) Technical Line

*Technical 2-year line: Clothing Manufacture; Food Processing; Workshop; Motor Engineering; Woodwork; Building and Construction; Electro-Technical; Processing Techniques; Forestry; Agriculture; Gardening; Technical.

Although the Swedes are very preoccupied with the ideal of equality and open access to education their system has, in practice, been quite highly selective. This is because the numbers admitted to the courses in upper secondary schools are determined by the government in accordance with the expected manpower needs of the economy. Where there are more applicants than places, selection is made on the basis of school grades.

Thus, in the popular subjects — science, medicine, dentistry, agriculture, veterinary science, engineering and technology competitive entry is similar to that in most other countries, including Britain. However, in other subjects, a major effort has been made to 'democratize' higher education by abolishing the old matriculation qualifications for university and, instead, allow anyone who has completed his or her upper secondary education to enter university.

The outstanding feature of the Swedish system, however, is the very large number of adults who return from a period at work to resume studies in the upper secondary school (which includes our further education colleges) and in university. In 1974, the proportion of university students who were mature workers reached 40 per cent of the total of 16,000 new entrants.

By the end of the decade, when the university intake is planned to more than double, over half the students are expected to come from employment rather than school. Normal entrance requirements are waived for anyone over 25 who can show that he has been gainfully employed for at least five years before applying to university. Swedish research bears out the conclusion of the British Open University — that very many adults in the working population have the aspiration and the ability to gain good class university degrees, even though they failed to gain the formal entrance requirements whilst they were at school.

The wish to give adults the chance of personal academic development which they may have missed in the school system is, however, by no means the only reason for encouraging them to study. The Swedes have been among the first to recognize the importance of re-training in an advanced and developing country and, as a result, the majority of their upper secondary courses and many university studies have a strong vocational bias. New legislation passed in June 1975 (U 68) is intended to strengthen the vocational bias of higher education. It will put all higher education under the control of eight regional committees which will include strong representation from trade unions and the community. Only a third of the members will come from within higher education.

The U 68 Act will also increase the proportion of vocational courses from the present 70 per cent to 75 per cent so that only a quarter of Swedish 16 to 19-year olds will be able to take non-directed academic courses.

In any comparison between Britain and Sweden, it is important to remember two facts; first that Sweden is a relatively small country and secondly that it is considerably richer. The sweeping reforms have, inevitably, been expensive because the Swedes have recognized that the more progressive approach is more difficult and requires more teachers, better equipment and more training. The attempt to provide a more egalitarian system by deferring selection has meant that children stay longer at school. Better vocational training has also meant longer schooling with an inevitable increase in cost. The relative rapidity of changes and tight central control have been made easier by the small size and relative homogeneity of the population.

As a context to more detailed discussion of some of the points of comparison of the Continental system of education with our own, a few more general points need to be established.

Private Education in Europe

The importance of private enterprise and private benefaction in establishing the British education system has been immense. The great independent schools have, for centuries, dominated the secondary education scene as the objects of admiration and envy. Year after year, the Labour party renews its pledge to abolish them and as often decides that it would be impractical to do so. The objections to our private schools are in proportion to their success (they still provide nearly half the students for Oxford and Cambridge). Because of the enormous prestige of our best independent schools, most Englishmen consider private schools to be a peculiarly British conception.

This is far from the case: the proportion of children educated privately in Britain is actually smaller than in many other countries.

In France, where 17 per cent of children are educated privately, private schools produce a quarter of the candidates for the *baccalauréat* — the university entrance examination. Since 1959, all private schools have been eligible for direct state subsidy provided that they comply with national standards of curriculum and enrolment. As a result of the 1959 law enacted by President de Gaulle, 95,000 of the 116,000 teachers in private schools have their salaries paid by the state.

In Holland, the state subsidy of private schools is complete. As a

Table 2

Numbers of pupils and students in European Countries (1970) (Millions)				
	Compulsory Schooling	Primary	Secondary	Higher Education
France (1970)	8.5	4.8	3.7	0.80
Germany (1971)	8.2	4.1	4.0	0.63
Netherlands	2. 23	1.46	0.77	0.246
Sweden (1973)	1.01	0.704	0.310	1.40 approx.
UK (1971)	9.17	5.93	3.25	0.45
Japan (1971)	14.2	9.5	4.7	1.66

Source: OECD Statistical Year Book, 1974.

25

result, 72 per cent of primary schools, 71 per cent of general secondary schools and 27 per cent of grammar schools and universities are privately owned. As in the case of the British voluntary aided schools, these private schools are closely integrated with the state.

Size

In making comparisons, it is important to remember the differences in population size between the countries. For, in the generally expanding populations since the war, education policy has been very much a scramble to provide the basic necessities of schooling for more and more children. This has been very much the case in Britain where the population has only recently started to fall. France, Germany and the UK can all be grouped together as having comparable populations whilst Holland and Sweden are very much smaller. The whole of the Swedish compulsory school population is, for example, only of the order of that of Greater London.

It is obvious, at once, from table 2 that the proportion of students in higher education compared with the numbers in compulsory schooling is considerably smaller in the UK than in other countries. This is a reflection of two facts: first that we restrict access to universities whereas our Continental neighbours have traditionally not done so and secondly, university courses in the UK are much shorter, lasting only three years compared with up to seven in France, Germany and Holland.

Our education should also be considered in the context of total population and income levels.

A rough idea of the total volume of education provided by different countries can be obtained from Table 4, which illustrates the percentage of the population at various ages receiving education.

Table 3

	Population (Millions)	Average income £ per employed person (1973)
France	52.1	5,800
Germany	62.0	6,600
Netherlands	13.4	6,950
Sweden		
UK	56.0	3,500
Japan	108.2	4,380
Source: *The Common Market and the Common Good,* EEC.		

Table 4

		Age 16	Age 17	Age 18	Age 15-18
Percentage of population at each age group enrolled at the beginning of the year cited.					
France	1970	62.6	45.1	29.1	54.3
Germany	1969	30.8	20.4	15.7	30.5
Netherlands	1970	60.6	41.5	28.4	52.5
Sweden	1972	74.0	60.8	40.8	68.1
UK	1970	41.5	26.2	17.6	39.4
Japan	1970	79.0	74.8	29.9	65.8
Source: OECD Educational Statistics Year Book, 1974.					

Table 4 shows quite clearly that, at the beginning of 1970, Britain was well behind other countries, except Germany, in encouraging young people to stay on at formal schooling. And it is interesting that in three countries where the staying-on rate is markedly higher, Sweden, France and the Netherlands, secondary schooling has been given a very strong vocational bias.

Expenditure

Whether educational expenditure can be regarded as a national investment with a direct economic return is one of those chicken-and-egg problems to which there is no conclusive answer. In the 1960s, the fashionable assumption among educational economists was that there was a direct link. A casual look at the high educational expenditure in developed countries like Sweden and the USA seemed to suggest a connection which was argued in detail by Professor John Vaizey (now Lord Vaizey) in his book, *The Economics of Education.*

Lately, however, economists, including Lord Vaizey, have doubted whether high spending on education may not be as much a result as a cause of economic growth.

Even a brief comparison of Britain with German would seem to confound the simple view that pumping money into the educational system is a necessary precursor to high economic growth.

For Germany has spent relatively little on education and has kept a system which is still based on pre-war tradition and structures. Although the Germans are now increasing educational spending quite rapidly, the effects on the economy can scarcely have worked through yet. Britain, on the other hand, spent considerably more on education throughout the 1960s than either France or Germany but is now lagging behind economically.

The expenditure pattern can be seen from Table 5.

Table 5

Public expenditure on education (current and capital) in $ Million at official exchange rates 1960-1970				
	1960	1965	1968	1970
France	1,467	4,058	5,614	6,911
Germany	1,680	3,410	4,137	6,475
Netherlands	529	1,200	1,757	2,362
Sweden		1,256	2,104	2,530
UK	2,857	4,953	5,602	6,893
Source: OECD Educational Statistics Year Book 1974				

III. Primary and Nursery Schooling – The Early Years

Throughout the 1960s, the British educational establishment basked in the glory of the primary school revolution. Experts from all over the world made their pilgrimages to see the new methods in practice and were directed to the finest of our pioneering schools. Education professors, teachers and administrators came and often marvelled to find that it really worked.

In many of the new progressive schools, like Prior Weston in the rebuilt Barbican area of London, they found that the traditional idea of a formal timetable with set lessons and a defined body of knowledge had been blown away by the gusty vigour of new theories. Children were freed from the arbitrary interruptions of the timetable, to follow their aptitudes and interests. They were free from the boring routines of parrot learning to absorb facts and to develop skills in the natural rhythm of their own enthusiasm; they were freed from the forced march of a uniform syllabus to dart ahead or retrace their steps according to individual ability; and above all, they were freed from the nervous stress of competition — they now worked as individuals or in small groups instead of being paced by the whole class.

And the results seemed good. Mr John Blackie, former chief of Her Majesty's Inspectors for Primary Schools, says in his book, *Changing the Primary School* (Macmillan, October 1974):

> The first and most important change was an enormous increase in the writing output of children at every stage. Whereas ten-year-olds in the 1930s would perhaps fill one or, at most, two exercise books a year (and this represented their total output) children of the same age nowadays write many hundreds of pages. Children astonished their teachers by the amount they wrote, if given the chance, and by the interesting content of their writing.

The opening up of the curriculum was accompanied by the opening up of classrooms themselves. Mr Blackie describes the new approach to space:

The doors will often be left open and, if there is a corridor outside, the children will overflow into this and find more space for their activities.

It is true he cautions:

These physical changes in themselves will achieve nothing but chaos and uproar!

But, like many propagandists who have helped to change our schools, he vaults lightly from practical advice to visionary zeal. He says:

The justification for recommending the progressive approach is that there is no evidence that the traditional one is proving so successful that it clearly ought to be retained and there is reasonably good evidence, based on research as well as experience, that the progressive approach is more suited to what is known of the children and their development and produces better all-round results.

But this measured practical tone changes abruptly and he goes on:

The writer's opinion is that the progressive approach treats children and teachers as persons, as individual souls if you prefer it, to a greater extent than the traditional. It allows greater place for love, both in the sense of the Greek *philia* and in that of *agape* and is therefore more in harmony with the vision of human happiness which still *brightens our dreams however much it may elude our grasp.* (Author's itals.)

With such propagandists to help, the British primary school, or at least the best examples, became for a time the admiration of progressive educationists throughout Europe.

But after the pilgrims returned to their own lands, they were slow to change established ways. In France, Germany and Holland primary schools remained much the same as they were: to British eyes, they increasingly appeared old-fashioned, formal and inflexible. They retained many of the characteristics of the pre-war British system and even, it was hinted, of the Victorian Board Schools.

Children sitting in orderly rows, learning in unison, chanting tables, remembering by rote and repetition, formal — often stilted — compositions and a grammarian approach to language; these were the overt characteristics of the majority of Continental primary schools. And, indeed, the formal style of teaching is still to be found in most of them.

There were, however, three other differences which reinforced the traditional approach in Continental Europe. These were: first, the stronger powers of central bureaucracy; they tied teachers' promotion prospects much more to a conformity with central norms of teaching behaviour than in Britain. There was little prospect of progressive teachers clustering into groups under a sympathetic Chief Education Officer as happened, for example, in the West Riding of Yorkshire under Sir Alec Clegg.

The second restraint was that European countries imposed a curriculum on schools, administered centrally, as in France or regionally, as in Germany. Alternatively, teachers were given some freedom of method but subject to strict control of standards, as in Holland. An imposed curriculum made change to thoroughgoing progressive methods impossible, while imposed standards made it risky for teachers. In all these countries there have been limited experiments with progressive teaching but they have been regarded by governments as no more than experiments and fairly strictly circumscribed.

The third restraint was the practice of making children repeat a grade if they failed to reach the prescribed standard at the end of a year. Grade repeating is still widespread on the Continent, although efforts are being made to reduce it. The practice points to a fundamental difference of approach from Britain where, even in the most traditional schools, children will move up a year however low their standards.

Grade repeating is a consequence of the idea that progress through school is by means of a staircase of which every step is a fixed standard. Any child who cannot reach it must wait on the step below until he has improved.

This system was rejected in Britain because it was considered inefficient as well as cruel. It can be inefficient because children, forced to repeat a year, become bored and dispirited and are, therefore, likely to fall even further behind. It is considered cruel to brand children as failures because they do not meet an arbitrary standard. In reality, children represent a spectrum of abilities rather than just the two categories of those who move up and those who stay down or *bleibsitzen.*

In spite of these disadvantages, the Europeans have considered the system of grade repeating necessary to maintain standards and to provide incentives to work hard (and teach well). In the past, it is estimated that between 30 and 50 per cent of Dutch children were obliged to repeat a grade, although the incidence is being progressively lowered. In Germany, the OECD examiners reported in 1972 that 3 per cent of primary school children were repeating grades while the incidence in *gymnasium* and *realschule* was 7.3 per cent and 5.5 per cent.

In France 13 per cent of primary school children are repeating grades and 7 per cent of secondary children. By grade seven, some 40 per cent of children will have repeated at least one grade. *(Education in France,* André G. Delion, Paris, 1973).

In Sweden, the position was until recently broadly similar with some 8 per cent of children repeating grades.

The regime which produced the present generation of young French adults was characterized by a very high drop-out rate described by Dr W. D. Wall *(Constructive Education for Children,* UNESCO Press, 1975). He gives figures for 1963-64 which show that, in the first year of primary education (6 to 7-year-olds), 33 per cent of children were retarded by a year or more. But, by the age of 9 to 10 the number of pupils retarded by at least a year had risen to 51 per cent. He comments:

From these figures — which are probably typical of
Europe, it is possible to infer that failure as represented by
inability to conform to the standards set by the school
programme is very much more widespread than would be
expected from the known proportions of the dull.

Criticism of a system of standards with a high in-built failure rate
have been backed by studies which show that grade repeating has
proven counter productive. Instead of overcoming disparities among
children they have tended to perpetuate them. Since the disparities often
reflect regional or socio-economic causes the system cannot be
tolerated.

French Government figures show, for example, that the repetition of
grades is twice as common in Strasbourg (22 per cent) as in Nice (10 per
cent) and that the majority of children who repeat grades are from
farming or working class homes (44 per cent).

A study by A. Haramein of 17,000 children in Geneva *(Perturbations
Scolaires,* Delachaux and Niestle, 1965) showed that by the fourth year
(age 10 to 11), 34 per cent of boys and 27 per cent of girls were a year
behind. The proportions of backward children increased steadily as they
got older, while the proportion which was a year ahead steadily
reduced. Failure among these children was very clearly linked with the
socio-economic group.

In spite of all these disadvantages, the grade system is still the rule in
European schools, although there is now a move towarde more open,
flexible methods, this is cautious and limited. The French, for example,
introduced 'active methods' into the primary school in 1969 but only as
a supplement to formal instruction. Teachers are no longer told
precisely what to do each lesson but they are still obliged to spend ten
hours a week on French, five on mathematics, six on cultural disciplines
(history, geography, singing, painting etc.) and six on physical
education. While reforms on the actual curricula are being considered,
emphasis on basic skills is simultaneously stressed. Modern
mathematics, for example, has only been introduced in the last four
years and then only in combination with the acquisition of more formal
calculating skills.

In Germany, the *Bildungsgesamt* plan of 1972 provided for
experimental projects in the discovery methods, which have only just
ended their first phase. It recommended a general move towards
progressive teaching in primary schools but the plan has been accorded
a mixed reception in the *Länder* and, because of objections to its over-
progressive tone, the commission which produced it has now been
disbanded.

In the conservative *Länder* like Bavaria, schooling is still strongly
traditional although in large cities like Berlin and Hamburg there is
more awareness of progressive attitudes.

The Dutch, under the leadership of Dr Jos van Kemenade are only
now planning a move towards more active and individual teaching
methods. Of all the European countries, the Swedes have travelled

furthest along the progressive road, but the primary sections of their comprehensive schools still have many of the features of the traditional system.

Among British experts, the fashion has been to deplore the faults of continental primary schools and to assume that, sooner or later, they must follow the trail blazed by our modern teachers. But before slipping into this assumption, it is also worth considering the advantages of the continental methods and whether they have not, in some respects, served their countries well.

It is especially interesting to consider the example of German schools because they have been represented as being, in many ways, the most old-fashioned and the most repressive. Education spending in Germany has been at a lower level than in most other European countries since the war (this is now being reversed). Classes were, therefore, larger and selection for *Gymnasien* (grammar schools) was fiercer. The pupil/teacher ratio in German primary schools was 1:37 in 1970, compared with a ratio of 1:27.7 in British schools *(Education Statistics,* HMSO, 1973) and in 1963 only 14.45 per cent of 13 year-olds could get to grammar school. (Saul B. Robinsohn and Helga Thomas: *Differenzierung im Sekundarschulwesen,* Stuttgart: Klett, 1968). Thus classes were far too big for informal methods to be possible while stiff competition for secondary schools made parents very wary of any change which might threaten standards in a particular school. Parental discipline has also backed up a strict and often successful regime in primary school. The first examination is at only 6-years-old — the *Schulereife* test to discover whether the infant is ready to start primary school. Those who fail twice are likely to go to a special school. The child then faces continuous examination and assessment by teachers to determine whether he has made the grade or must repeat a year. The assessment of his teachers will also play a large part in determining whether he is selected at 10-plus for *Gymnasium* or *Realschule.*

Those who fail to be selected, stay on in the upper division of the primary school, the *Hauptschule* which is still, in many areas, part of the all-age *Volkschule.*

These pressures undoubtedly produce casualties, a considerable amount of stress and unhappiness with even a sprinkling of child suicides.

Nevertheless, the Germans have achieved a truly amazing increase in prosperity since the devastations of the war and it is more than probable that their primary schools have contributed to the atmosphere of hard work, discipline and respect for excellence that is one of the main strengths of German society and German industry. It is hard to doubt that the competitiveness and the ambition which the primary schools systematically reward, have helped industry to be successful, whatever one may think of the intrinsic desirability of these characteristics.

Another point which the British should note at a time of worsening discipline in schools, is that German teachers manage to keep good order without the use of the cane. And this is not simply because of stronger parental control. One reason for good discipline, in spite of large classes, has been the system of grade repeating which gives teachers a very important sanction. German children know that their teacher has power to promote or demote them at the end of the year. This may be a much better incentive to buckle down to hard work than the vague threat of corporal punishment.

One further point is that a central or regional curriculum may, in spite of being restrictive to some teachers, give help to those who are weaker or less experienced. It frees the teacher from the worry and hard work of determining what to teach and allows him to concentrate on the practical job of getting it across.

Finally, although German schooling has been criticized widely and not least by the Germans themselves, for excessive rigidity and for failing the less able, it has, with relatively little cash support, given efficient grounding to a majority of the average and clever. It has done this, moreover, with a system of half-day schooling which leaves the whole of the afternoon free for play or individual homework. What the children make of their free afternoons obviously depends on their parental background. The more deprived children clearly suffer but, where the the parents' support is good and the children well-motivated, half-day schooling can have important advantages. In particular, it stresses the need for parental encouragement (which is vital in any system) and it introduces early habits of independent work.

The picture in France is similar, although classes are smaller; the disadvantages of over-formal methods and the effects of formal primary school teaching have been recognised earlier and mitigated by an excellent and nearly universal nursery school system.

All five-year-olds, 85 per cent of four-year-olds and 75 per cent of three-year-olds are in nursery schools. These schools use the same informal learning through play techniques as the majority of British infant schools. This means that, although compulsory schooling starts a year later than in Britain, the majority of the children will have completed three years of informal learning before they begin at the primary school. Furthermore, the best of French nursery schools have a sharp educational purpose and experiments are now being made on laying the foundations of maths, French and a foreign language — even in the nursery classes.

By contrast, nursery education in Germany is under-developed, including in 1970 only half the five-year-olds. The General Education Plan hopes to bring the standard of provision up to that of France by 1985. In Holland, 82 per cent of four-year-olds and 95 per cent of five-year-olds are in nursery classes. In Sweden, day nurseries for children aged one to seven of working mothers' are provided for 40 per cent and nursery schooling for four to six-year-olds for 30 per cent.

In Britain, where provision of nursery schooling has lagged behind, much of the preparation undertaken by the continental *Kindergarten* is deferred until children reach the infant school. By 1980, we shall be providing half-time nursery places for about 70 per cent of four-year-olds and 40 per cent of three-year-olds, which will still be below the provision in France. A French child may well start two years earlier and experience teaching methods at least as informal and progressive as in the majority of British infant schools. Against that background, the greater formality of the primary school seems more logical. A similar point can be made about Sweden where primary schools start two years later than ours.

There are several reasons, therefore, why the British disdain of European primary education may be misplaced. But perhaps the most important reasons for ending our former complacency are internal: a growing feeling of unease about standards, the realization that progressive schooling is not the panacea its apostles have sometimes represented it to be and an understanding that new methods make teaching more difficult rather than easier, so that in some cases, teachers cannot adequately cope.

The national complacency was first punctured by the 1972 reading tests (National Foundation for Educational Research) which were part of a routine monitoring exercise, commissioned by the government. After testing 7,150 children in 300 schools, the Foundation concluded:

Reading standards are no better today than they were a
decade ago and, in one respect, have declined since 1964.

The tests showed that, between 1948 and 1961, reading standards of 14 year-olds improved by nearly 20 months' reading age but, since then, the improvement had stopped. Interestingly, the researchers found that the standard of the middle-ability range had been maintained but there had been a fall in the standard of the top 30 per cent and of the bottom 40 per cent of children. This finding appears to support the critics of progressive, mixed-ability teaching, who have repeatedly pointed out the danger that cleverer children may not be stretched and that duller pupils may find working on their own too difficult.

The NFER said:

The 11 year-old who score half-way between the highest and
lowest scores in 1970 is six months behind his 1964
equivalent. The very bright 11 year-old is three months
behind and the weakest 10 per cent is three-and-a-half
months behind.

The report also found that one in 30 of the 15 year-olds measured in 1970 could read no better than the average nine-year-old in 1938. It said:

Compared with 1938, there is the possibility that there has
been an increase in semi-literacy of both juniors and seniors
and in the illiteracy of juniors over the last six years.

Critics immediately pointed out that there had been sampling problems due to a postal strike and the apparent reluctance of some schools to fill in the forms; the tests were showing signs of becoming out of date with some archaic words and constructions and there was a high rate of absenteeism among the early school leavers tested.

However, the researchers considered these difficulties and concluded:

> There is no reason to assume that any resultant distortions
> induced by these factors should have necessarily been mainly
> in one direction or should render invalid inferences that are
> made with due caution.

The Bullock Committee set up by Mrs Margaret Thatcher in the wake of the NFER controversy did little to resolve the issue. It came out with a lengthy and heavily qualified statement of the progressive consensus with a strong note of dissent from a traditionally-minded headmaster. The committee repeated the NFER figures with caveats and pointed out that the big rise in standards in the 1950s was only to be expected after the disruptions and evacuations of the war. The report did, however, conclude that standards of literacy needed to be improved and it provided some 600 pages of helpful advice on how schools should achieve it. The committee recommended better arrangements for monitoring standards but rejected all proposals for controlling them.

These figures are among several factors which have led to a change of public mood. During the 1960s the optimism of leading progressives was generally shared by most sections of the public: many parents found their children were happier with the new freedom and, if they were a bit confused by some of the new methods of teaching, they were generally reassured by the message of confidence which came from the teachers' spokesmen, widely relayed by the national and local press.

In the last few years, however, that general buoyancy has given way to doubt, disappointment and controversy. The doubts were first voiced by the educational *Black Paper* in 1969. At first, this document by academics and teachers was treated with disdain by much of the educational establishment mainly because of the polemical style of some of the contributors. But *Black Paper One* also contained a powerful and carefully reasoned criticism of the excesses of progressive methods. It was written by a distinguished and respected professor of education, G H Bantock, of Leicester University. This article set a new style of scepticism for informed opinion so that the hot gospellers and the enthusiasts began to meet concerted opposition for the first time.

Middle class opinion, which had generally supported the new methods, began to waver as increasing numbers of parents complained that children 'were not learning their tables', were 'playing around' and 'could not spell'. At the same time, there were, and still are, many parents who enthusiastically support the new methods.

Disquiet over the effect of progressive methods on school standards in Britain has not been confined to parents: considerable unease within the teaching profession has been demonstrated in a very large volume of discussion on the subject in the professional press. Teachers' unions have repeatedly drawn attention to the extra demands which the new teaching imposed on their members. And in 1973, the National Union of Teachers produced a document urging more caution in the move towards open plan schools — the architectural embodiment of progressive teaching. Apart from detailed criticism of skimped materials and design, one of the main complaints was that open plan schools preempted important decisions about the way in which children should be taught. Architects had, in effect, assumed that the bandwagon towards informal group methods would continue to roll. Teachers were finding that, like it or not, they had to have up to 90 children in the main class under the charge of a team of three teachers. This forced a whole range of teaching techniques upon them because the design of the new buildings precluded traditional class instruction.

These doubts and arguments might have been surface ripples on the main stream of progress: plenty of people represented them as no more. But then in the summer of 1975, a progressive primary school suddenly exploded into the public notice. The minutest details of its working were exposed to the full glare of publicity. The result was first surprise and then shock.

It was a school with many advantages: it had one of the best staffing ratios in the country, generous allowances, a considerable influx of ambitious middle class parents in an otherwise working class area, a staff blending youth with experience and enthusiasm for progressive methods. It had a young headmaster with an excellent teaching record.

William Tyndale Junior School is only half a mile or so from the famous Prior Weston Junior School to which foreigners have made their pilgrimage in hundreds. The teaching methods were, theoretically, similar to those at Prior Weston. Many of the educational principles advanced by its headmaster would have graced a manual for progressive teachers. Yet, instead of becoming a source of national pride and foreign envy, William Tyndale School became the subject of public enquiry and of indignation throughout the land. The first symptom of failure was that about 100 parents removed their children because they believed they were not being taught reading, writing and arithmetic properly. Their fears were borne out by evidence at a public enquiry that children were allowed to play during lesson time; that table tennis and party games were part of the normal school curriculum and that indiscipline, ignorance and abuse among the children were the results. A report by the local inspectorate said:

Many of these children of nine or ten were unable to use a ruler, spell the simplest words, to write more than a few sentences or even to form their numbers and letters.

The inspectorate met with temper, tantrums, sulkiness and obscene language among the pupils. Even though their report was undertaken in the unusual circumstances of a strike by all but one of the teaching staff, they found many highly disturbing attitudes. Some children refused even to go into a classroom.

Children were apt to be unkind and rude and potentially dangerous acts of violence had, at times, to be suppressed.

The inspectors commented, significantly:

It was also evident that (the children) became increasingly responsive to the normal techniques of class control as the period of the visit advanced.

They also said:

> Some first year children displayed marked symptoms of
> regression resulting from lack of security that must be
> deeper than the effect of the relative upheaval caused by
> the absence of their normal teacher.

The inspectors were charged to make a sober appraisal of the school;
they represent an authority which is generally sympathetic to the
progressive approach, yet there are passages in their report on William
Tyndale which are an uncanny echo of the polemical warnings of the
Black Paper writers five years earlier. The significance of the Tyndale
enquiry was not, however, to show that modern primary school
methods can turn sour. That could easily be predicted.

What shocked many people about the exposure of William Tyndale
School was not that the headmaster had taken progressive teaching too
far; it was the revelation that he was at liberty to experiment with his
new methods and curriculum with almost total freedom from constraint
by the school's managers, the inspectorate and the authority who all
lacked the power to make him revert to more acceptable teaching.

Although many of the circumstances revealed by the William Tyndale
enquiry were peculiar to one small, bad school, the proceedings
attracted immense public interest because they were, in a sense, a trial
of the whole British primary school system. They revealed to the world
that, while boasting of having some of the best primary schools in
Europe, we were also nurturing some of the worst.

The complacency which led the British to despise, or merely ignore,
the primary school system throughout Europe may justly give way to a
humbler spirit of enquiry, for there cannot be any doubt that the
breakdown at William Tyndale would have been impossible in France,
Germany, or Sweden. More seriously, the William Tyndale teachers
displayed a casual, even contemptuous, attitude to established school
standards quite alien to the beliefs and practice of continental schools.
Their suspicion or rejection of traditional standards is, moreover,
shared by a considerable part of the British teaching profession. It has
bred a confusion about the objectives of primary schooling which
continental teachers do not generally share. And this rejection has
penetrated to the innermost fastness of Her Majesty's Inspectorate, the
body which once guarded, but now says it guides, the standards of our
schools.

Mr. Blackie says:

> It would certainly be possible to undertake a comparative
> study of achievement in the three Rs of two groups of
> schools, one avowedly traditional and the other avowedly
> progressive but even this would prove very little. What
> would be measured, though important, would be too little.
> Suppose, for example, that the traditional group scored
> more highly in spelling than the progressive group — it
> would still have to be shown (and this would involve a
> value judgement) that this deficiency was not compensated
> for by other unmeasured and possibly unmeasurable
> achievements, such as width and quality of reading, powers
> of conversation and social awareness.

Mr. Blackie describes, in this passage, something of central importance to British Primary education which is still obscure to most of the public and to some teachers: the progressive revolution does not simply concern *methods*; it represents not just a better way of mastering the old skills of the three Rs; it entails different objectives, which are sometimes radical, often unmeasurable and almost always, unmeasured. The change poses the question: do we want good spelling and adding or social awareness?

The new objectives have not recently been discovered: developing 'powers of conversation and social awareness' were the aims of good teachers before Socrates. The novelty is in the emphasis and the style, which may prove to be of the greatest importance to the way our children develop and to the very foundation of future citizenship. For Mr. Blackie considers, and he may be right, that consensus about the traditional aims of education is now destroyed. He lists some of these former aims: 'to arouse in children a respect for democracy'; 'to train children to be loyal to King and country'; '. . . to help children to understand the government and institutions of their country and thus learn to respect them'; 'to bring up the children to be Godfearing and obedient'.

But he rejects them all on the grounds that trying to secure agreement about such aims is a hopeless task in modern Britain. He says:

. . . some of the aims listed above are incompatible with
the progressive approach with which this book is
concerned. An approach which encourages children to
think for themselves, to ask questions, to co-operate will
not also encourage them to accept, unexamined, the society
in which they live and its institutions; nor will it encourage
an unthinking iconoclasm.

Because this is half-true, it needs to be challenged. For Mr. Blackie is presenting the classic liberal argument between freedom and authority as a false dilemma; critical thinking is not incompatible with loyalty to the Crown, with obedience, the fear of God or, indeed, any similar aim. The fact that these aims have been associated with authoritarian regimes is no more an argument for rejecting them than was the inquisition an argument for despising Christ. Furthermore, the connexion between progressive methods of education and critical thinking of real substance should not be overstated. It is teachers, not methods, which produce alert thinking and if progressive methods give more opportunities to the best teachers, they also give more scope to the worst.

As the old consensus among teachers and the public has been destroyed, progressive teaching has simultaneously introduced new aims as well as new methods into our schools. The important question for policy-makers is, therefore, whether the determination of aims as well as basic standards should be left almost entirely, as at present, to the teaching profession and, in many cases, to individual teachers.

Do we want a society of good spellers and accurate arithmeticians or a generation of imaginative enthusiasts? Do we want people to work because of a habit of discipline or only when they are motivated? Should we try to encourage our children to accept society and feel patriotic pride in its past and its future or should they be taught to question every aspect of our social and religious beliefs?

It is an error of dogmatists in the extreme progressive as well as the traditional camps to present these questions as stark alternatives, whereas the best teachers steer a middle course. Nevertheless, these extremes do indicate the way in which different teaching approaches will have different effects in determining the kind of people we hope our children will become.

They are questions which, in continental Europe, the community as a whole attempts to decide but which, in Britain, have been allowed to drift. A return to strict central control of standards, formal teaching and a system of grades would be unacceptable to the teaching profession and probably to many parents. It would also run counter to the European experience. But if the continentals are moving in our direction, they are not rejecting all traditional practices to anything like the extent that has happened in some of our schools. Their example and indeed the observations of many experts in Britain, point to the need for combining formal and informal methods.

All other countries have some outside method of assessing school standards. Indeed, the eleven-plus crudely performed this task although it was never designed to be a monitor of the whole range of ability. The disappearance of the eleven-plus has left a gap through which the standards in some schools can imperceptibly slide. The danger is now partly realized by the Department of Education and Science which in January 1976 set up an advisory council for an Assessment and Performance Unit, whose task will be to find new ways of monitoring school standards and practice. In the absence of any political initiative, however, the unit is unlikely to make a very strong impact on schools in the foreseeable future.

While, therefore, the French, the Germans and the Dutch are considering a cautious reform in the direction which we have travelled, it may be appropriate to ask whether the British should not move back to meet them in the middle ground.

The most important evidence in support of those propositions was provided by a major research study by Mr. Neville Bennett of Lancaster University *(Teaching Styles and Pupil Progress,* Open Books, 1976). After careful testing of children in 37 different classrooms where different teaching styles were used, Mr. Bennett discovered that traditional teaching produced better progress in almost all aspects of childrens' work. Not only was there improvement in spelling, mathematics and reading but, more remarkably, the progressive methods failed to produce the often claimed superiority in imaginative or descriptive writing.

His report shows that progress was better in all schools, formal and informal, where the eleven plus examination still operated than in those where comprehensive education had been introduced. Children in the informal classes were more anxious than those in the formal classes. The researchers watched all kinds of classes in operation and concluded that children in the formal groups spent much more of their time on 'work orientated' tasks than children in informal classes who tended to chatter to each other.

Critics have made much of the fact that the best teacher in the study was using broadly 'progressive' methods. However, the crucial observation was that, although her methods were informal, her teaching was highly organized. It is an exception which proves the rule in an interesting way; for it illustrates that progressive methods can indeed produce excellent results when they are employed by a skilled, well organized and hard working teacher. The error of enthusiasts like Mr. Blackie is to assume too readily that the informal techniques can be adapted successfully by middle-of-the-road teachers.

Mr. Bennett's research has helped to quantify the bewildering variety of aims and methods in primary schools. He provides some reassurances that all schools have not gone overboard for informal methods. According to his survey, about one teacher in six is using the progressive approach. On the other hand, there is little doubt that the general climate of opinion has been moving rapidly towards the more informal methods, so that some schools now considered to be traditional would, 20 years ago, have been classed as 'trendy'. Above all, the report enters a plea for a more measured, better researched approach to change which has been notably absent in the last two decades.

He says:

> As far as primary education is concerned, this 'giddy chase' (after new methods) has consisted in running around in circles. Education would seem as prone to change in fashion as clothing . . . It would seem clear that, on both sides of the Atlantic, innovation is being urged without research. This, of course, is not new in education, the common response being that education decisions cannot wait for years while careful trials are instituted and evaluated. Yet it is a strange logic which dictates that we can afford to implement changes in organization and teaching which have unknown and possibly deleterious effects on the education of the nation's progeny.

Improvement of standards, depends, in the view of the teachers' unions, on further expenditure on yet more teachers, equipment and buildings. Others, including the James committee on teacher training and the Bullock Committee, have emphasized the need for a big increase in the re-training of teachers already in the schools. These remedies can be ruled out until at least the end of the decade because of the need to stabilize public expenditure. In any case, there are indications that pumping more money into the system may not be the answer. The Education Priority Area experiment set up in 1968 by the late Mr. Anthony Crosland, yielded disappointing results. The intention was to find ways of improving educational standards in deprived areas by special programmes and extra money. The gains were, however, small and the report on one project *(Educational Priority Volume 3, 1975)* came to the astounding conclusion that a progressive programme using a large amount of extra money and extra teachers actually had negative results. The children ended it with a worse standard than they would have achieved with ordinary schooling.

It is obvious, therefore, that new ways must be sought for securing the desired improvements; the most obvious is to provide schools with more overt guidance about the standards expected, to give teachers incentives for achieving them and to introduce a national monitoring system to find out what is happening to children.

Teachers, and particularly the National Union of Teachers, have objected that such measures could hamper the progressive approach. But the example of Sweden shows that the setting of national standards and national tests in primary schools need not be inconsistent with a fully comprehensive modern approach. There, a national curriculum, introduced in 1972 (Lgr 1969) includes progressive style teaching by the project method, a modern approach to mathematics and individual work by pupils. Yet achievement tests are given to children at 9.5, 12.5 and 13.5 years and thereafter at yearly intervals with half-yearly tests in the upper school. These are supplemented by diagnostic tests at 6.5, 10, 13 and 16, although there are current proposals to abolish these tests from the *Betygutredning* committee. Criticism is directed against their role in selecting pupils for academic courses rather than their function as a monitoring of standards.

In Britain, the present proposals for testing are only on the basis of 'light sampling' which will give a rolling result for overall national standards but will say nothing about the individual achievements of schools or pupils. Universal testing has been rejected because of objections from teachers and progressives who say it would restrict teaching developments and reinforce the sense of failure of less able children.

These objections have some force although, as has been made clear, there are arguments against giving unrestricted freedom to teachers. However, the objections could largely be overcome if testing were in the first place voluntary and to some extent anonymous. If testing were voluntary, schools which opted out would then be obliged to justify to managers and parents the different methods or curriculum which made testing inappropriate.

Alternative testing could be partly anonymous so that only the school authorities knew the results of individual children. The public would have access to generalized results for an authority or a school and parents would be given the results of their own child to compare against the norms where appropriate. Such a system could avoid the individual distress which could result from the publishing of lists of performance at too early an age. Some people argue that it is better to face facts by openly quantifying the differences in attainment which most children are, in any case, aware of. The objections to public testing are those encountered in the eleven-plus in Britain and the assessment tests in Sweden. The objection is that, because of inherent crudities, tests may wrongly condemn a child and that a child wrongly marked down may give up hope or be written off by his teachers.

Research, as well as experience, indicates that a child who is discouraged too early can suffer a bad reverse or even a severe trauma; but fears of this type are often exaggerated because they are associated with the selective purposes of the eleven-plus. In a system which, for better or worse, will soon be fully comprehensive, the primary schools will be freed from the anxieties as well as the spurs of selection.

It should further be observed that, in schools which allocate children to different ability streams, grading already occurs so that objective tests will merely provide more information about children who know they have already been assessed. In a progressive school where all abilities are taught together, a national test need make little difference to the child's own evaluation of his progress but it would provide important information to the teacher about individual pupils as well as the standing of the whole class in relation to national norms.

More generally, testing would provide a reassurance for the public if, as progressives maintain, standards are improving. If they reveal areas of weakness, the public will also be reassured that the deficiencies can be known very much more precisely than at present. The vague observation of the Bullock Committee that people have always complained about standards is, clearly, no comfort to an influential section of industry or to many parents.

More controversial than testing, is the question of whether any parts of the curriculum should be imposed on schools. The two are linked for if, as in Sweden, there are national tests of standards, detailed curricular guidance may not be necessary as well. And if, as in France, you have a fairly detailed instruction on the curriculum with standards for each grade, the assessment of individual pupils can be left to the teachers.

In Britain, which has neither, a cautious introduction of assessments in basic skills at ages 7, 10 and 14 might be enough. However, there is a strong argument for trying to find a national consensus about a basic core of knowledge and skills which children should all be taught. At least if consensus is impossible, the points of difference would be defined. What relative weight should be given to mathematical and literate skills for example? Should ability to calculate be given priority over other mathematical skills and, if so, what is the minimum calculation skill which should be required of an 11 year-old? Should all children know the basic outline of the history of their country and the geography of the world — to what extent can 'environmental studies' provide a substitute? These are the kinds of question which are of national importance and it seems odd that we should allow different answers in almost every school.

A great deal of parents' present anxiety is the result of not knowing what answers their local school has formulated to such a question —

and in some cases, there is a strong suspicion that the local school has not even formulated the questions. For progressive teaching can too often avoid the hard intellectual challenge of defining what, at the end of it all, the children are expected to know. This may be particularly true of inexperienced teachers carried forward on a tide of enthusiasm which has insufficiently stressed the difficulties of the new techniques.

National guidelines need not be binding on schools — few people would like to emulate the rigidities of the French or German systems — but they could, by their mere existence, exert a powerful influence. An outline curriculum, agreed by a commission of teachers, industrialists, citizens and academic experts would, at least, provide a reference point for parents or administrators. This is, in effect, the procedure adopted in Sweden with the difference that the curriculum agreed becomes obligatory.

The British tradition of freedom would not easily accept this. However, under present legislation, local authorities could be asked to prepare curricular guidelines for the help of their schools and the government could set up an independent commission in co-operation with the authorities to give a national context to their work.

If this were done, it would be a simple step to require head teachers to explain publicly to parents their reasons for any divergence from the national or local guidelines. The guidelines themselves need not cover the whole of the school timetable or curriculum, so that some areas of absolute discretion would still be left.

This system would represent a mild form of control compared with that in other European countries. It would safeguard the traditional freedom from direct government manipulation of school courses because the national committee would be independent and advisory, executive power would rest, as at present, with the local authorities while the government would, as at present, place general duties upon them.

The system would deter the more half-hearted progressives and provide a means for curbing the most extreme. It would provide a lever for improving specific subjects like mathematics which are now generally acknowledged to be badly neglected. But, at the same time, teachers using sound progressive methods which carry the support of parents and their authority, would have freedom to continue to develop, experiment and prosper.

IV. Secondary Education –
The Search for Equality

Throughout Britain in pubs, clubs, offices and at select dinner parties people are arguing about comprehensive schools. Some politicians on the left say the argument is now over because more than two million of the 3.5 million secondary school children are now in comprehensives *(Statistics of Education 1974,* Vol. 1 HMSO). By 1980, the present government plans that almost all grammar and secondary modern schools shall have been reorganized as comprehensives or closed. But, although comprehensive schooling will soon be a *fait accompli* for the majority of the children, the argument shows no signs of abating. Indeed, the Conservative Party has recently mounted a more vigorous defence of 'good schools' and has tried to organize opposition to the encroachment of the comprehensive principle into counties like Buckinghamshire, where the local authority does not want it and to the voluntary grammar schools whose governors would like to resist it.

The present war of words and emotions over the future of comprehensive education is very different from the smooth progress towards the ideal of equality which seemed assured in the 1950s and 1960s. Then, many Conservative, as well as Labour councils, were eager to abolish the hated eleven-plus examination. The emergence of the argument about comprehensive education at the turn of this decade was fuelled by disappointment with some of the results; the unexpected problem of size contributing to poor discipline and a flagging morale; shortages of specialist teachers and instability in the profession which produced very low standards in some departments of some schools; the publicity given to a few outstandingly bad schools in large cities and anxiety by the middle classes that comprehensive schools were rejecting the basic social and academic values which they wanted for their children. The current debate is often based on a fundamental misunderstanding about secondary schooling and comprehensives which the Labour party progressives have helped to spread with their propaganda against academic selection and their proclamations that they intend to abolish it.

As a result, many people are forgetting the rather obvious fact that all secondary school systems are selective; they always have been selective and, in the foreseeable future, the majority of them will remain selective. This is as true of Sweden, where a fully comprehensive system has been established for 15 years, as it is in countries like Germany and Holland, which have different schools catering for different aptitudes and abilities.

Selection is necessary because not all children can go to college or university. Therefore, at some stage in their secondary school careers, some children must follow more academic courses than others. Even rich countries like the USA and Japan, which provide higher education for a majority of children, have not abolished academic selection though they have, to some extent, postponed it. Experience of comprehensive schooling in the USSR and in Sweden shows that selection can be postponed to 13 or 15 but, in Sweden pupils need to spend a longer time in the upper secondary school and at university than they do in Britain.

Much of the present debate in Britain is clouded by a failure to come to terms with these essential facts. The real question is not *whether* to select pupils for more difficult courses but *when* and *how* to do so. Most feasible methods of selection are now being used in different parts of Britain and the range of possibilities is so wide that the differences within comprehensive schools are at least as great as the differences between comprehensive and the so-called 'selective' system. Unfortunately, a preoccupation with abstractions like 'equality', 'social justice' and 'academic excellence' has often diverted attention from the practical consideration of how a comprehensive system should be organized. One consequence is that too little thought has been given to ways of preserving the best of the grammar school tradition within the new system.

In some schools, children are divided into separate streams from the first so that the old divisions between grammar school and less academic styles of education are largely maintained. In others, children of all abilities are taught together up to the age of 14 or even 15 because it is thought that mixing all abilities together is the only way of making a school truly 'comprehensive'. Some continue to teach in a traditional academic way, whilst others, particularly those which mix abilities, are experimenting with a whole array of new techniques and types of course. Individual schools have been allowed to follow their own paths, to a large extent, though unlike the primary schools, they are subject to the restraints of public examinations at 16 and 18. The changes have been made with little reference to any lessons which could have been learned from our European neighbours (except Sweden). It may have been assumed too readily that the French and German systems are fiercely selective. Whilst this is true in most of Germany and Holland, it is certainly not true of France, where the move to comprehensive schools has been more rapid than in Britain, though it started later.

French *collèges d'enseignement secondaire* were started in 1963 to bring all 11 to 16 year olds into the same establishment. By 1973, 65 per cent of children were in the new institutions and the changeover is now more-or-less completed. At first, children were divided into three separate streams, the *lycée* stream corresponding to the old grammar school education, the CEG or *collèges d'enseignement général* stream corresponding to a secondary modern style of teaching and a third stream for remedial education. Proposals by the Education Minister, M. Haby, early in 1975, to abolish the three streams in favour of a common course for all children, ran into strong opposition from parents and teachers. They were first abandoned but later re-introduced in a modified form.

The first two years of the French comprehensive schools are designated as an observation phase in which there is a common curriculum so that children can be moved between different streams. Selection for the different streams at age 11 is made on the basis of primary school teachers' reports and on the profile of school marks obtained by the pupil. Selection is also made, in practice, by grade repeating or grade jumping. This allows a bright child to jump a year ahead, while a dull child may be up to two grades behind. Further selection occurs at 16 when entry to the upper secondary schools is competitive.

It should be noted that the existence of defined grades and a standard curriculum means that even the progressives' proposals to integrate the three streams would not mean that all pupils would progress at the same rate. It would mean that they would progress up more similar ladders at similar speeds.

In the Soviet Union, where all children are supposed to follow the same course in unstreamed schools up to the age of 15 (eighth grade) about one fifth of the pupils are unable to maintain the pace. Some repeat grades twice, or even three times so that grade repeating is a concealed selection. Selection also happens by three other means: a system of elective special courses for bright children from the age of 13 (grade 7) upwards, competitive examinations at age 15 for the most popular secondary polytechnic schools and competitive entry to the special schools for the academically gifted which are now being developed. (There are eight such schools in Moscow and others in Leningrad, Kiev and Novosibirsk) *(Paths to University,* Arthur Hearnden, Schools Council 1973).

A similar pattern of selection by ability within a comprehensive system can be traced in Sweden though the mechanisms are rather different.

In Sweden, as in the Soviet Union, comprehensive schools embrace the whole of the primary and lower secondary stages of education from 7 to 16. But at 16, Swedish children must face competitive entry to one of the three types of upper secondary education: the *Gymnasium* (academic school) providing three year courses leading to university, the *Fackskola* (continuation school) offering less theoretic more vocational courses; and the *Yrkeskola* (vocational school) for mainly two year full time apprenticeships. These three types are now combined in the

Gymnasieskolen but the distinction between the three courses remains. Up to grade six (age 13), all children are supposed to follow the same programme in unstreamed classes. At age 13 they choose between a series of options which give the brighter children a chance to study an extra foreign language for five periods a week; the duller pupils opt for five periods of handicrafts and there are intermediate options with a more or less academic bias. By the age of 14, more options are introduced and, at fifteen, the children are allocated to the *Gymnasium* stream or one of eight other streams. In principle, children and their parents are allowed free choice between options but, as the number actually admitted to the *Gymnasium* section of the upper school is limited, the advice of teachers carries a great deal of weight. Thus the Swedish comprehensive system has had an inbuilt selective method starting at 13 with competition for grammar school-type of education at 15. And although the recent proposals aim to give equal value to all lines of study in the upper secondary school (age 16 to 19) the effects on childrens' chances are still problematic.

In Holland, selection to different secondary schools is still mainly by competition based on examinations and school grades. The same is true in Germany but attempts have been made to mitigate the arbitrariness of selection at 10-plus by giving parents a large measure of free choice. In Germany, if the primary school agrees with the parents' choice of school, no examination is necessary. If the parents refuse to accept the primary school's recommendation, they can ask for an examination and, even if a child fails, it is still possible for the parents to insist that the child should be admitted to the school. As a result, most children whose parents want them to go to a *Gymnasium* or *Realschule* are admitted. However, the standards of the schools are quite strict, so that a child who fails to make the grade after the first two years (age 12) will be transferred downwards. Consequently, parents will often take the advice of teachers if their child is clearly not suited to an academic course.

It should be obvious, therefore, that the ideological difference between comprehensive and selective schooling is not always as great as has been assumed.

Few people in any country now favour a simple once-and-for-all selection at eleven-plus. On the other hand, even in Sweden, a selective process starts at 13 and is quite marked at 15. Indeed, it is one of the paradoxes of comprehensive schooling that the selective pressures *inside* an institution can be greater than in a system where children compete for different schools. The extreme case is Japan where the Americans imposed a comprehensive system on to an elitist tradition after the war. As a result, all Japanese children attend the same type of comprehensive school up to the age of 16 and follow basically the same curriculum. The aim was to promote equality and the Japanese still proclaim proudly that they have a system of complete equal opportunity. Same school, same course for all — so each individual has the same opportunity to succeed, they say.

The result, however, is a fierce rat-race which begins in early primary school as children struggle, grade after grade, to keep ahead of their peers until the all-important examination at 16-plus for the upper secondary school. Only the best of the upper secondary schools send many pupils on to Tokyo and the handful of other top universities. In the absence of a selective examination at 11, the school grades do a great deal of weeding out of the slower pupils and, as a result, one of the main talking points in Japan today is how to ameliorate the 'examination hell' into which they have thrust their children. The high and increasing rate of suicides among young Japanese children is attributed, partly, to the enormous pressure of their comprehensive school system.

In the comprehensive schools in Sweden, the adoption of a common course and imposed standards has led to similar pressures, though they are, perhaps, not so acute as in Japan. These pressures led progressives to demand in August 1975, an end to the system of school marks (Times Educational Supplement, 8 August 1975). However, although this may postpone selection by allowing some pupils to follow courses to which they would not otherwise have gained admission, it is difficult to see how it can make a very great difference to the realities facing children. As Stuart Maclure has pointed out in the TES (April 1975), the amount by which a country is prepared to postpone selection is dictated to a great extent, by economics. The USA can afford upper secondary education to the age of 18 for the great majority of teenagers (as can Japan) and about half of the age group now goes to college. Standards are, however, inevitably lower than in this country; to reach the equivalent of our upper sixth form standard, many Americans have to spend two years at college. This is obviously more expensive. Even if such an arrangement were desirable, it is not likely to be economically feasible in Britain for many years to come.

These comparisons do no more than indicate that the theory of comprehensive schooling must be approached with great caution, for the schools are by no means a panacea even for the 'evil' of academic selection which they were created to abolish. The realities of selection should be considered as much within schools as in the system as a whole, for it is defined largely by the chance a child has of progressing to an academic course and of subsequently entering university or college. These figures are given in Table 8.

The figures show that the chances of getting into a university are broadly comparable in continental Europe with Germany and Holland rather behind and France ahead. The British figure is rather better than it appears because our different system ensures a lower drop-out rate; so that although relatively fewer get a university place compared with France, the British student has a much lower chance of being thrown out after the first or second year.

The outstanding point to emerge from the table is the very considerably greater chance of higher education in Sweden, roughly twice as good as in Britain at the university stage. This fact must be

Table 8

Proportion of age groups in upper secondary school academic courses and proportion going to university and higher education. 1970				
	Proportion doing academic Sixth form work	Per cent of age group in higher education	Per cent non-university higher education	Per cent of age group going to university-type higher education
France	25	22.4	7.4	15.0
Germany	17	15.8	5.4	10.4
Netherlands		18.3	10.0	8.3
Sweden	30	37.6	14.2	23.5
UK		20.6	10.0*	10.6
Japan		23.9	7.0	16.7

*Excludes 66.2 thousand block release, day release, evening course students. If they are included, the proportion rises to 18.6 per cent.

Source: OECD Statistical Tables 1974

borne in mind in any comparison with our own system.

The amount of selection is, therefore, determined mainly by the opportunities provided for school-leavers and not by the system itself. The methods and age of selection will vary considerably between different comprehensives but, by the age of 13 or 15 at the latest, the majority of pupils will be firmly placed in different academic paths. The bland fiction that comprehensive schools are 'non-selective' has distracted the attention of policymakers from the highly important question of how and when it is desirable to differentiate between children. Only the most extreme progressives deny that this is necessary; for it is neither kind to pupils nor desirable for society that children with low academic abilities should struggle with the academic courses suitable for future university students.

Granted this point, the question is: at what age should a different sort of course be available and how different should it be? Solutions vary from school to school but, because comprehensive schools are generally pledged to an egalitarian ideal, the tendency is to put off the choices for less able pupils and to give them courses in the image of those for their academic peers. Courses for the less able are at best 'relevant' to their experience and interests and practical in orientation. The worst are merely watered-down academic study with little obvious value to anyone. And, in most courses, there is a bias towards personal and general education.

Efforts to avoid selection in comprehensive schools have thus tended to produce a uniform, general type of education rather than a choice of vocational options.

The Swedish comprehensive schools up to the age of 16 do much the same but the important contrast with Britain is that the upper secondary school choices are highly differentiated and include many courses leading directly to particular trades and professions. Our comprehensive schools have not generally developed anything like such a variety of courses. The main reason is that, unlike the Swedish upper secondary schools, they are quite separate from the technical colleges which provide the bulk of vocational training. Our comprehensives are thus cut off from the training requirements of the majority of pupils to a much greater extent. This point will be expanded later. For the moment, it is enough to observe that by putting the selective pressures *inside* our schools, we have altered the type of education given to pupils in ways which may not have been intended.

Comprehensive Schools and Equal Opportunity

If comprehensive schools cannot ultimately prevent pupils from being selected for different types of study and eventual occupations, it was hoped, at least, that they would provide a fairer means of doing so. It was argued that children would be able to transfer at a later stage of their development between different sorts of courses. In practice, however, these ideals have been difficult to realize. The earliest comprehensives in Britain placed children in different streams according to their primary school reports. In theory, children could be promoted to a higher stream but, for two reasons, the movement was not great. The first was that children tended to perform to the level expected of their stream, even where tests showed that they were more intelligent than their classmates. The second obstacle to free movement was that schools were naturally reluctant to demote many children from the upper streams. Demotion had a depressing effect on pupils and provoked opposition from parents. Consequently, the number of vacancies for promotion into the upper streams tended to be limited.

The alternative is varying degrees of mixed ability teaching. This means that pupils work at their own pace with the help of individual programmes and graded work cards. Even where this method is successful, and it puts enormous extra demands on teachers, there is often a tendency for the abler children and those from more educated homes to benefit disproportionately compared with those of lower ability. It is difficult to generalize because the success of this method varies greatly with the ability of the teachers. However, it can be said that, in cases where mixed ability teaching is not properly prepared, the results can be so chaotic that the children from the poorer homes have little chance of moving up the academic ladder.

A further difficulty is that comprehensive schools in middle class neighbourhoods inevitably draw a greater proportion of children from families with an academic tradition and academic ambitions than schools in working class areas; some schools thus become 'academic' schools while others will remain 'non-academic' and the differences will be reinforced by the type of teachers recruited.

These arguments are supported by the available facts which indicate that comprehensive schools themselves are unlikely to do much to make educational opportunities between classes more equal and, indeed, they may make opportunities less equal. In Sweden in 1972, only 10 per cent of working class children went to university, compared with 20 per cent of lower middle class and 80 per cent of the upper middle class.

When the Swedish comprehensive schools were developed in 1968, the immediate effect was that those who were already favoured became more favoured still. As Professor Sixten Marklund, Professor of Education at Stockholm University, observed:

Students from the upper and middle classes who had
previously been excluded because of inadequate
qualificatons were the first to seize the opportunity when
the intake restrictions were done away with. Similar effects
have been observed in other countries following the
broadening of admissions to secondary schools. (TES, 14
March 1975)

More recently, Swedish government surveys have shown an increase in the proportion of working class children going on to higher education but this has probably more to do with the enormous expansion of the provision of schooling and higher education rather than with the specific comprehensive pattern. It is clear that a country which provided upper secondary schooling to the age of 18 for 80 per cent of pupils and university places for nearly a quarter of them will make educational opportunity more nearly equal, however it is organized.

In the European context, Britain has promoted social equality through education as well as or better than most other countries and there is evidence that, whatever the objections to selection at eleven-plus, the old grammar schools did a reasonably good job in this respect. The Robbins Committee in 1968 estimated that the proportion of students from working class homes was 25 per cent.

This figure appears not to have changed greatly since then *(A Fresh Look at Higher Education,* Jack Embling, Elsevier, 1974). Comparable percentages for other countries in 1968 were:

Sweden	14.3
France	9.4
West Germany	5.9

(Walter L Buhl, *Schule und Gesellschaftlicher Wandel,* Stuttgart: Kett 1968 p.34).

Precise comparison of percentages is open to question because of the different ways of making social classifications. Nevertheless, the figures indicate that social mobility in British higher education is certainly no worse and probably a good deal better than in other countries.

Mr. Embling, who has wide experience as a member of OECD and

UNESCO commissions says (op cit):

> The lack of any uniform classification makes it impossible
> to make any precise comparison between the situation in
> Britain and in other Western European countries or to test
> the dubious claim that British universities have a higher
> proportion of working class children than those in the
> others. What is clear, however, is that the situation in all
> countries is much the same.

Further evidence that comprehensive schooling does not, necessarily, promote equality can be seen in the USA where the US Bureau of Census found, in 1970, that of all families which included one dependent member aged between 18 and 24, only 16.6 per cent of those with an income under $3,000 had a son or daughter in college, compared with 66 per cent of those with an income of over $15,000.

In Britain, the comprehensive schools have not been established long enough to make any great impact on social mobility. However, there is certainly no indication that they are improving the statistics of educational opportunity. The proportion of entrants to Oxbridge from state schools compared with public schools has recently started to decline after a steady increase since the war. The proportion of pupils getting GCE 'A' Levels is now static or declining. It was 17.8 per cent of all school leavers in 1973-74 compared with a peak of 18.4 in 1971-72. And, at the same time, demand for higher education has declined so that the number applying for university is well below the forecast of the Department of Education and Science based upon the trends of the late 1960s.

It is now generally accepted that as a means of promoting social equality schooling is a factor which has been much over-rated. Mr. Embling says (op cit):

> The papers prepared for the OECD Conference (Policies
> for Educational Growth 1970) show that inequality, far
> from diminishing with the expansion of higher education
> and higher education expenditure has, in many countries,
> increased. For it is the non-manual classes which have
> exploited the extra opportunities. In other words . . . the
> remedies for socio-economic disparities lie in social and
> economic policies and not in education.

In other words, if you want people to have equal incomes, the best way to do it is to give them equal incomes and not equal education. And if you try to give people equal education, all the evidence points to the probablity that sons and daughters of educated parents will tend to benefit proportionally faster than those from less educated families. The fact that the USSR and China have found it necessary to operate quota systems in favour of the working classes, lends further support to this proposition.

The consequence for the debate about comprehensive schools is that reorganization is much less important for the egalitarian aims of the left than the present government has suggested. There is certainly no firm evidence that comprehensive schooling will, by itself, improve the educational chances of working class children and, in some respects, it may hinder them. There are good arguments, therefore, in favour of a slower, more experimental approach, particularly in view of the current shortages of specialist staff, of suitable buildings and money. These arguments are reflected in changes of attitudes of teachers who, in the 1960s, were generally in favour of comprehensive reorganization. In 1974, however, a National Opinion Poll survey commissioned by Times Newspapers, showed that 77 per cent of primary school teachers and 67 per cent of secondary school teachers favoured the retention of grammar schooling. Furthermore, two out of five Labour voting teachers opposed their own party line on the issue *(Teachers and the British General Election 1974,* Times Newspapers).

Comprehensive Schools and the Curriculum for the Less Able

The development of comprehensive schools has meant a longer period of general education of a more-or-less academic type for the average pupil. This has happened in the USA, the USSR, Sweden and Japan and it is now happening in France and the UK. In all these countries, the trend is for largely similar lessons to be given to all children up to the age of 15 or 16. There are two reasons: the first is the general belief that the majority of children can and should benefit from four to five years of secondary education and that the aims of broadening the mind and extending the critical faculties previously reserved for the elite can be extended much more widely. The second reason is that any differences in curriculum inevitably produce academic selection and thus cut off future options for those who follow the less demanding courses. As early selection runs counter to the whole idea of comprehensive schools, teachers have tried to run courses which are as similar as possible for the able and the less able. In all other countries, these curricula are regulated by central authority but, in Britain, they are the result of teachers' local efforts and, therefore, vary greatly. However, a national pattern has emerged because of the development since 1968 of the Certificate of Secondary Education controlled by teachers through the 13 regional boards. From the start, the CSE was intended to be different from the GCE 'O' and 'A' Levels which are run by eight boards, mainly dominated by the universities.

The intention was to free that new exam from the outside control of universities and to provide courses designed to fit the needs of the pupils as the teachers saw them. Under the new Mode 3 system, individual teachers could, if they wished, design their own courses and carry out the assessment of their own pupils with only the supervision of an outside moderator to keep an eye on the standards. The result has been a proliferation of different courses and examinations. Some are in new or unusual subjects but the bulk of them reflect at lower intellectual levels, the general academic aims of the GCE 'O' Levels. Considerable overlap has been necessary because teachers have had to prepare mixed groups of pupils for the two examinations at the same time. Indeed, it is now proposed that the two exams should be merged together and the Schools Council has published a study which has been taken to show that the merger is feasible as well as desirable.

Few would argue against the need for a substantial core of general education up to the age of 16 but the concentration of efforts into the CSE has meant that the case for a more substantial proportion of vocational studies in the early secondary school has often been overlooked. Furthermore, a certain snobbery has developed against teaching children specific skills like typing, carpentry, plumbing or mechanics compared with developing more general knowledge and awareness. It would be unfair to imply that these subjects are not taught. They are, but too often they are on the fringes of the general curriculum rather than a central part of it.

The system of vocational schooling after the age of 11, of which the Dutch have been very proud, would generally be considered too elitist in this country. We are moving much closer to the Swedish idea of giving everyone, as near as possible, the same education up to 16. It is worth noting, therefore, that the Swedes are growing more and more aware of the disadvantages of the system. As Torsten Husen, Professor of International Education at Stockholm University says *(The Learning Society,* Methuen 1974):

> In consequence of the changes that have taken place, an even larger proportion of young people are growing up without any real contact with the world of work which undoubtedly constitutes the essential part of adult existence. The prolongation of childlike dependence on home and school to the late teens and the problems associated therewith, have been specially accentuated by the fact that physiological puberty among today's urban youth sets in almost two years earlier than it did 50 years ago. The keyword in all the curricula that have been drawn up in Sweden during the last two decades is 'fostering': fostering personality, fostering responsibility, independence and co-operation. Such glamorous words have been strewn by generous hands at planning sessions and teaching seminars and have helped to frustrate many teachers by further underlining the discrepancy between theory and blank educational reality.

Professor Husen describes the ways in which teenagers are becoming more and more cut off from the realities of society, except by the second-hand means of television and similar filters and he comments:

> I believe that one of the most over-riding problems is how young people are to be given opportunities to learn meaningful things and not to be deterred by the teaching to which they are exposed, for all its good intentions. The phrase 'good intentions' is well-advised in this context because it strikes me as infinitely tragic in many cases to observe the ambition that inspires the vast majority of teachers — particularly in the secondary schools — and the disappointment they feel when they cannot attract the interest of their pupils. We are then told that teaching doesn't get across because discipline is bad. A question less often asked is whether the menu offered to the pupils is to their taste.

These comments can be taken as a fairly sharp warning about the way in which British education is heading. In some respects, we are worse off than the Swedes, whose upper secondary schools, the *gymnasieskolan* for 16 to 19 year-olds have integrated the technical colleges with the more academic types of education. Pupils are thus presented with the option of 20 different lines of study, many of which have direct links with particular occupations and vocations. Recently, these links with work have been strengthened by the tendency for more and more teenagers to leave school at 16 or 17 but to return after a period at work.

The proportion of 16 year-olds moving directly into the upper school has declined from a peak of 75 per cent in 1971 to 65 per cent in 1974. At the same time, the number of upper school students has continued to increase because of adult enrolments, so that the numbers now correspond to 93 per cent of all 16 year-olds.

The latest proposals from the Schools Ministry's Project Group (January 1976) are aimed to strengthen links between work and upper secondary schools by allowing the pupils to study part-time, on the same basis as adults. And a full government-sponsored enquiry is to investigate ways of achieving suitable courses for the whole range of 16 to 18 year-olds.

The Swedish comprehensive school system thus recognizes three distinct but related purposes: first, the need to select or guide pupils of high academic potential towards university; secondly, the need to give all pupils a common general education; and thirdly, the need to provide a large variety of differentiated courses leading towards different occupations. In Britain, the comprehensive schools have been set up without much guidance from the national government or often from the local authorities about how these different aims should be pursued. Different schools have searched for their different ways to salvation or, in many cases, they have just muddled through.

The comprehensive schools have been hampered by the fact that they are, in one important way, not fully comprehensive. This is because a great deal of the education of teenagers between the ages of 16 and 19 takes place, not in schools but in different colleges with different staffs, different regulations and, very often, a markedly different outlook. This separation is, probably, even more important than the separation from the academically best schools (the direct grant and voluntary aided grammar schools) to which the left wing has drawn attention.

A West Indian teacher in a comprehensive school with a large proportion of immigrants, described the difficulty in this way:

Academic standards are very low and many of the pupils
do not try because they think they have no hope of
competing in the academic race. As a result, they become
bored and frustrated and they lose all their pride. They
think they are no good and they think they will never get
decent jobs or succeed in society. We need to give them
skills that they could be proud of. If the boys were taught
to be good motor mechanics they would see that they could

get good jobs perhaps, eventually, own their garage and rise in society.

But the school does not teach motor mechanics or other vocational skills in an organized or thorough manner. Its main efforts to meet the needs of black pupils has been to devise courses in Black studies and try to find other ways of making school 'relevant'.

This is not to argue against Black studies or any other attempts to try to relate school courses to the experience and interests of particular pupils. The point is, simply, that teachers have too often been forced to search for the ways of making subjects 'relevant' to pupils who should really be doing something else altogether. A course with a different vocational purpose will often provide the direct relevance to a pupil's interests and ambitions that more general studies lack.

The growing trend of teaching all children together in mixed-ability classes is further obscuring the need for schools to exploit the different interests and abilities of children to the utmost, rather than trying to obscure these differences to a later and later stage. Mixed-ability teaching inevitably means that all children follow essentially the same course although, ideally, the cleverest study faster and deeper than the others. Only the most brilliant teachers can provide enough genuine variation to suit all types of children in one class.

Comprehensive Education — a Summary

The majority of British secondary age children is already in comprehensive schools, and even if some of the best selective schools are preserved, they are likely to be in a small minority quite soon. Careful thought is now needed about how to preserve the best of the grammar school academic tradition within the comprehensive system. The solution in France has been to divide comprehensive schools into three distinct streams, the upper stream corresponding to the old lycée type of education. Efforts to promote equality of opportunity have been concentrated upon providing flexible opportunities for transfer between the streams. The first two years are designated as an observation phase with a common curriculum for all children. The intention is to defer final selection to the age of 13. More recent proposals aim at increasing the possibilities of transfer up to the age of 16.

However, the French system recognizes the vital importance of operating academic selection within the comprehensive schools while, at the same time, every effort is made to ensure that it will be as fair as possible. The official guide to French education (*Education en France,* op cit) says:

That tough selection should be the absolute rule of every sane community, no sensible man would dispute. But it is necessary that this selection should operate on realistic criteria and, after having given pupils a range of chance to succeed in different ways.'

Similar sentiments underline the cautious approach of most of the

German provinces to the question of comprehensive schooling. The Federal Plan for Education which envisaged a progressive move towards comprehensive schooling, has been rejected by six of the eleven provinces *(Länder)*. The majority of comprehensives *(Gesamptschule)* are on the French model with separate streams while those which are completely integrated are still regarded as experimental and are surrounded by controversy. In 1973, only 121,000 or 2.5 per cent of German secondary school pupils were in comprehensive schools. The majority of these schools are in the province of Hesse which had, in 1974, 117 comprehensive schools, of which only about half were integrated like British and Swedish comprehensives. There are now no plans for more comprehensives until the present 160 experimental schools have been evaluated. Unlike the British, the Federal German Education Council decided to precede the general change to comprehensive schooling with a limited experiment programme of 40 comprehensive school pilot schemes. Although some successes have been claimed, the results are far from reassuring. The official German publication *Bild und Wissenschaft* comments: (BW 8-1974) that criticism which had previously been confined to grammar school teachers and more conservative groups has now broadened to include former sympathizers, comprehensive school teachers, pupils, parents and education researchers.

It reports:

There are increased signs among pupils of disinterest, in school, absenteeism and destructiveness, a lack of discipline and agressiveness.

and

The fluctuation of teachers is remarkably high with fewer replacements coming from volunteers.

In an article in *Westermann's Paedagogische Bietrage* (No. 3, 1974) Hans-Karl Eckmann describes the numerous reports of resignations and discontent among comprehensive school teachers, which he attributes to the enormous over-burdening of work and the increasing 'ideological accentuation of the teaching body'.

The Germans have met the familiar problems of how to teach the clever and the dull together and maintain standards at the same time. *Bild und Wissenschaft* comments:

Curricular problems, such as giving body to the fundamental framework of basic learning material, compulsory for all pupils, and the supplementary range of pupils who learn faster, are still unsolved and are likely to be solved only after years of development.

it concludes:

At the moment, unanimity exists only on the fact that a basic model for the comprehensive school cannot, and should not exist and that this is a 'progressive reform' which prepared for long periods of developments and that an entrenchment or freezing of development, as the result of too much planning, would be harmful.'

Even the left wing have become disenchanted: Carl-Heinz Evers says in *Betrifft: erziehung* (No. 3/1974 pp 45-47) that the idea that comprehensive schools would provide 'compensatory education' has proved to be an idealogical illusion. He attributes the comprehensive school crisis to a contradiction with the demands of a capitalist society He says that an attempt must be made to analyse whether this type of school is possible at all in a capitalist society and, if so, whether comprehensives could themselves help to bring about anti-capitalist changes.

In Sweden, in spite of the bold conception and the detailed thoroughness with which comprehensive school reforms have been introduced, there are still major problems: including alcoholism and drug taking, now spreading from the three major cities. A national poll in 1970, nearly 20 years after the first comprehensive schools were established, revealed that the reform was widely regarded as a failure — with 78 per cent of parents dissatisfied. The actual classroom methods in unstreamed groups have led to widespread reports of boredom among pupils and, in spite of having the best staffing ratio in Western Europe, the Swedes still have a grave problem of illiteracy. A research study by Hans Grundin of Linkoping Teachers College *(The Development of Reading and writing Ability throughout the School Years,* Liber Laromedal, Stockholm, 1975), found that about 15 per cent of 16 year-olds leaving the comprehensive schools had a reading standard well below that of the average 13 year-old, widely regarded as the minimum level needed in an advanced society. Furthermore, 5 per cent of 16 year-olds had reading and writing skills which were well below those of the average 11 year-old. He commented:

My study has indicated that thousands of young people leave
school in Sweden every year without having reached the
rather high level of reading and writing ability our society
expects them to have reached. This is a serious problem. To
try and remedy it can be regarded as one of the most
important tasks of our comprehensive schools.

The public reaction to this survey has been alarmed and rapid with demands for extra programmes to ensure that pupils master the basic skills.

The Swedes are also increasingly concerned about the rate of mental illness among school children and the alarming number of children who commit suicide. Many factors in society may be responsible but doctors believe that schools are among them. Mr. Stig Palsson, school doctor for the Stockholm county and one of the country's most respected experts, estimated in his report in 1974, that more than 3,000 of the county's 129,000 comprehensive and secondary school children needed psychiatric help. Mr. Palsson himself estimates that these figures very considerably underestimate the problem. His report particularly sites the high drop-out rate from schools — about 10 per cent, or 100 per comprehensive school with 1,000 pupils — as one of the causes.

Many of the problems encountered in Sweden and elsewhere have been reflected in Britain and it seems odd that so little attention was given to international comparisons when we were setting up our own reforms. The French, for example, decided in 1973, not to build any more very large schools of more than 900 pupils. This was just about that same time as the very great disadvantages of huge impersonal schools was being realized in Britain. By then, it was partly too late, for we had already built a large number of schools for up to 2,000 pupils and even more. However, in Britain as elsewhere, the basic decisions about comprehensive education have been taken, not on the pragmatic grounds of what would be educationally sound, but for broader social and political reasons. The OECD report on German schooling, which came out in favour of comprehensive reforms said:

The decision on whether or not to have comprehensive schools is, inevitably, a political one to be taken primarily on social or political grounds. Pedagogical or psychological experiments can, perhaps, help with certain technical problems of organisation and provide experience of new curricular arrangements. They will not tell policy-makers whether comprehensive schools are 'better' or 'worse' than selective schools, because a final judgement on that matter must depend on the weights placed on the various criteria employed. Such weights are inherently highly subjective.
(Germany: OECD, Paris, 1972).

The current education bill introduced by the British Labour government to compel local authorities to reorganize their schools, underlines the political nature of the change. Unfortunately, when an issue becomes political, people tend to see only the broader issues and ignore or falsify the detail. If Britain is to have a fully-comprehensive system, it is of the utmost importance to realize that the new system has inherent difficulties to which no country has yet provided a clear solution and that the hoped-for advantages are likely to be much less spectacular than was commonly supposed by the optimistic propagandists in the early 1960s.

1.   Comprehensive schools are internally selective. Muddled thinking on this point courts disaster.
2.   The belief that selection can be avoided by setting up classes of mixed abilities is fallacious: the degree of selection is determined by economic factors and particularly by access into higher education.
3.   Mixed ability teaching is unlikely to promote greater mobility. The 20-year experiment of Swedish comprehensives with mixed ability teaching up to the age of 15, indicates that children from poorer homes may even be put at a disadvantage.
4.   Mixed ability teaching puts enormous extra burdens on the teachers. Reports from the Assistant Masters' Association in Britain, from Germany and from Sweden — all indicate the same. Furthermore, the Swedes have encountered difficulties in spite of much more favourable staffing ratios, better research, a more homogeneous population and stronger central support.
5.   Teaching in mixed ability groupings *can,* undoubtedly, be successful

as schools in Britain and Sweden have proved but, it is important to be clear that the criteria for success should be precisely pedagogical and not social, political or vague.

6.   Comprehensive schools in general and mixed ability teaching particularly, are likely to exert a profound influence on the curriculum, with a tendency towards general and personal education rather than vocational studies. While in Sweden and France these changes are effected and regulated by a central decision, they will be determined, in Britain, by the drift of fashion and opinions among teachers. Comprehensive schools give teachers new choices and new powers about which there is little opportunity to formulate public policy.

7.   Comprehensive schools inevitably raise anxieties about the traditional academic standards especially when, in Britain as elsewhere, some teachers openly state that they see standards and attainments in non-traditional ways. In all continental countries, the standard curricula and defined grades or standards provide, in principle at least, some check on pupils' attainment. This function has been performed, in Britain, by the GCE Examining Boards and by teachers in schools.

8.   Proposals to merge the GCE 'O' Level with the CSE would effect a major transfer of power to the teachers, with considerable long-term implications. The proposed merger would allow schools to determine most of the curriculum for all children up to the age of 16. School standards would, certainly, become more relative than at present.

9.   The trend of opinion in Europe is now towards greater links between school and work in the upper secondary school stage. This, it is argued, is desirable to give pupils more incentive and also to give them better preparations for adult life. However, the continued separation of Further Education from the school system, makes this more difficult in Britain than elsewhere.

10.   In Sweden and France, the comprehensive principle extends only up to the age of 16, not to 18, as is usual in Britain.

None of these points needs to be an argument against comprehensive schooling in principle and, in spite of the various caveats, it is clear that the general trend in Europe is towards either comprehensive education or, at least, a greater integration of the separate types of secondary school. As already noted, France has almost completed this integration, while five of the eleven German *Länder* are pledged, in principle, to move in this direction. In Holland, too, the future is likely to see a progressive amalgamation of the large number of different levels and types of school. However, the methods of internal organization will be crucial and, in these three countries, the indications are that comprehensive schools will preserve the distinct streams for academic and less academic children. The difficulties of ensuring adequate transfer between streams are unlikely to be greater than those of organizing mixed ability classes.

Comprehensive education is in an unsettled state throughout Europe and, while so many questions about it remain unanswered, there are strong arguments for the British to proceed slowly and cautiously.

There is no evidence to warrant the belief that comprehensive schooling will provide such rapid or decisive benefits, either social or educational, that we need to make changes precipitantly. Particular caution would, therefore, seem prudent over any proposals to destroy good selective schools. The French have managed to incorporate their *lycées* into a comprehensive system for the post 16 age group. Similarly, the Swedes retained their separate *Gymnasien* in the upper secondary schools. There is no reason, in principle, why grammar schools should not have a place in some modified form within a comprehensive system. All the difficulties of staffing, discipline and morale in large 11 to 18 comprehensive schools, point to the need to reconsider the advantages of an upper secondary sector for the 16-19 age group, on lines similar to those in Sweden and in France. Such upper secondary schools, or sixth form colleges, can provide a concentration of staff which is not always possible in an all-through comprehensive and they will, at the same time, provide a second chance to the pupils who have the misfortune to go to a local comprehensive which is badly run. Otherwise, he may have no possible escape.

Much greater caution is also needed in the approach to changes of school courses and school organization. While changes may be necessary in the long run, much greater thought needs to be given to their implications by the public at large. Many of the changes which are now being made in British comprehensive schools are not, as teachers frequently pretend, merely matters for expert professional judgement. They will, cumulatively, make far-reaching changes in the fabric of our society and are thus of profound political importance. Britain is unique in having no organized means for public debate to influence or control these changes. The extent to which public control over what happens within schools is now needed, will be discussed later. For the moment, it seems reasonable to observe that organized continuous debate of the issue is desirable, practicable and not necessarily expensive. The alternative is to continue drifting and to hope that we may land somewhere — not too near the shores of chaos.

V. The Curriculum

That the product of education should be the educated man, may appear self-evident. However, when schools introduce the competing claims of greater social justice, personal fulfilment and the need to train for jobs, few things seem obvious and the obvious appears suspect. Thus a passionate search for new objectives and new significance has been started throughout Europe, particularly amongst educators who no longer suffer from the distraction of having to teach children. Their writings commonly use the words 'innovation' and 'improvement' as if they were synonymous and the most enthusiastic often seem to take it for granted that students should never be made to learn anything that they do not think they want to learn. Higher education courses in Britain have already been designed which allow students to write their own curricula (at Lancaster University and the North East London Polytechnic) and similar ideas are now at work in schools. The correct observation that people learn best what interests them, has sometimes led to the fallacious conclusion that it is pointless to expect anyone to learn what is dull. But, in spite of the blandishments of these new theories, most people still hold traditional ideas about the sort of accomplishments an educated man or woman should have. They believe the man should be literate, fluent, well-read, able to argue correctly, competent in a foreign language, acquainted with science and reasonably knowledgeable about the history and geography of the world in general and his country — not forgetting music, sport and art. This, or something like it, is expected of all intelligent boys and girls emerging from the upper secondary schools in France, Germany, Holland and Sweden. A full range of up to nine or ten subjects must be studied in the sixth form by anyone who wants to go to university. One obvious result is that most educated people on the continent, speak good English, while the English are notoriously bad at learning the languages of the foreigner — even including French, the main tongue studied in our schools. Less obvious, perhaps, is the fact that when

European teenagers reach university entry, they are much more versatile than their British counterparts. In principle, at least, the possessor of a *baccalauréat* or *Abitur,* the French and German matriculation qualifications, could enter any faculty that he wished. Recently, the pressure of applications has forced *numerus clausus* or competitive entry upon the most popular departments so that, to an increasing extent, specialization in the sixth form is being introduced. However, a French, German or Dutch 19 year-old with the school leaving certificate, still has a wide range of courses to choose from and, in many cases, he can choose between science or an arts degree at this late stage.

By contrast, the British pupil has often made choices of subject at 16, 15 or even 14 which may restrict his choice of university subject to a narrow range and may disbar him from the whole of science and technology. Early specialization is thus a major factor in producing empty places in science and engineering, which probably amount to some 6,000 places in universities alone, with as many again in polytechnics. Official estimates of the number of empty places were discontinued after 1974 because of protests from vice-chancellors that they gave a misleading picture. But there is no doubt that universities and polytechnics are working at well below full capacity in many of the subjects which have the most direct bearing on the nation's future prosperity.

By contrast, in Sweden, engineering and science and technology faculties have competitive entry like medicine, dentistry, agriculture and veterinary science. It hardly needs stressing that a country which is able to select future engineers and scientists from a wide field of sixth formers is likely to be in a stronger economic position, in the long run, than a country which has been forced progressively to lower entry standards in these subjects and is still unable to recruit enough teenagers to fill the universities.

Throughout Europe, there is unanimous agreement that the range of sixth form studies should include: mother tongue, a foreign language, mathematics, social studies (comprising history, geography, economics, politics and civics), physical and natural sciences and physical education. Because of the central control of curricula, it is possible to see precisely the relationship between time allocated to different studies.

The relationship has been tabulated by Arthur Hearndon (*Paths to University,* Schools Council, Macmillan, 1973) on p.65.

As can be seen, nearly 60 per cent of the course in France and Germany, and nearly half the course in Sweden, is given up to a compulsory common core. Between 8 and 16 per cent of the total time is given to mathematics and science and about the same for the minimum study of a foreign language. It is also worth noticing that *every* pre-university pupil in the USSR is expected to spend almost half his time on mathematics and science, a deliberate bias which is common to Communist countries, where industrial needs are given paramount importance.

Minimum percentage of total curriculum time given to common core subjects in upper secondary school				
	France	Germany	Sweden	USSR
Mother tongue	9	13	8	12
Foreign language	9	11	12	7
Mathematics	7	7	5	18
Social studies	7	12	9	3
Physical/natural sciences	8	4	3	28
Physical education	17	9	7	7
TOTAL	57	56	44	89

In Britain, a sixth former at the equivalent point in his education, may be studying only two closely related subjects — for example, physics and mathematics or English and History. It is true that the better 'A' Level candidate in the better schools will be taking three subjects supplemented by one or two non-examinable options, but other pupils may be taking a very narrow course indeed. Narrowness is a particular danger for the growing number of teenagers who leave school at 16 to study for their 'A' levels at the local technical college. It has always been argued *per contra* that the specialization of British 'A' Levels means higher standards in individual subjects. This is a necessary base for our concentrated three-year undergraduate degree course. It is also claimed that pupils' power of thinking can develop better through the detailed study of a subject at close quarters than through a frenetic tour of the whole of knowledge. Certainly, there has been strong criticism in Germany of the blinkered academicism of upper sixth form studies which, undoubtedly, depend more upon an encyclopaedic memory than on powers of thought. Drop out rates are high — only about 60 per cent of those who start the course eventually pass the *Abitur* without having to repeat a grade and many give up altogether. This is similar to the position in France where the *baccalauréat* has a 40 per cent failure rate — one fifth of those taking the exam are over 20. A broad curriculum, with the need to repeat grades also results in a high leaving age in Sweden where the average age is 20.2 years, though the high average in Sweden, is partly caused by the tendency for students to return to school after a period of employment.

As a result of criticism that the curriculum leading to the *Abitur* was too broad and too barren, the Conference of Provincial Education Ministers agreed, in June 1971, to a reform towards more specialist teaching. By 1973, 10 per cent of *Gymnasien* had implemented the reform, which allows pupils to choose two specialist subjects for intensive sixth form study. These and two further subjects are then the subject to the *Abitur* examination. This system of specialization is being imposed upon a common core curriculum which will continue to be assessed by the school's teachers, though the general load on pupils is being lightened. Hitherto, all *Gymnasium* pupils were required to learn no less than *three* foreign languages. Now there are courses which lead to the *Abitur* with two, or only one, foreign language.

Similarly, in Holland, everyone leaving the grammar school (*Lyceum*) who wants to go on to university, must take a leaving examination in seven subjects, two of which are optional and five compulsory. In all the streams, the compulsory subjects include Dutch and at least one foreign language (English, German or French). Many of the sixth formers take two foreign languages and some, three. In France and Sweden also, at least one foreign language is compulsory.

It is worth considering foreign languages more generally in relation to national needs. The Dutch, as a small trading nation with limited national resources, have always been forced to lay great emphasis on foreign languages. Since relatively few people in the world speak Dutch, learning and teaching foreign languages has been a vital investment on which, it is not too much to say, the country's very survival has depended. Similar considerations apply to Sweden while in France and Germany, cultural motives have, perhaps been mixed with commercial prudence. The fact is that every student in every university in Europe is supposed to be reasonably fluent in at least one foreign language, and often in more. Britain is the only country which allows, and even encourages, large numbers of students to drop the serious study of languages at 16 or earlier.

Dutch engineering students even have to read some of their text books and listen to lectures in English. Yet few British engineering students studied a language in the sixth form to examination standard; many have only a poor command of French. In the glorious days of the Empre, when trade with English speaking colonies and dominions was assured, the motive for learning languages was much less. But even in the last few years. Britain's economic position has changed remarkably. We now need to struggle for a living in competition as well as co-operation with our thrusting partners in multi-lingual Europe. Our school and examination system has made scarcely any response to this threatening new situation. A few attempts have been made to introduce courses in 'European studies' which may be of value in their own way.

Yet the obvious commercial need is to develop better linguistic competence amongst future administrators and managers. This can only be achieved by first, an insistence that languages are studied more generally in the sixth forms — at the very least, pupils should keep the mechanics of the language learned at 'O' Level in running order and not allow them to go rusty; secondly, a more practical approach to languages needs to be developed for many pupils. The emphasis should be on fluency and comprehension rather than the literary or grammarian approach.

Unfortunately, the teaching of languages, far from improving, is static or declining. The failure of the primary school experiment in teaching oral French has already been mentioned.

Inadequate standards amongst the primary school teachers, over-optimism about the benefits of tape recorders and film strips and lack of continuity with courses in the secondary schools were among the defects.

The teaching of languages in comprehensive schools is now running into similar difficulties. The spreading of abler pupils amongst an increased number of schools has led to a shortage of specialized language teachers. In addition, language staff have discovered great difficulties in teaching their subject to classes which have wide ranges of ability, including some children with an inadequate command of English and little enthusiasm.

Professor Harry Rée, the distinguished former headmaster of Watford Grammar School, discovered this for himself when he left his chair in Education at York University to teach French at Woodberry Down Comprehensive School in London. His comments have a special interest because he has still been a leading supporter of comprehensive schooling and is still optimistic about its future. After his first year of teaching a mixed ability group of 11 to 12 year-olds, he concluded that the exercise was impossible and that French should be made voluntary at least after an initial 'taste'. Professor Rée found that the more traditional approach needed for foreign language teaching did not fit in with the modern informal methods used in other subjects. One reason was that the children had no previous knowledge of foreign languages so that it was impossible to relate the subject to their own environment and experience as is attempted with, for example, mathematics and English. The other problem is that very good discipline is required: 'In order to understand a modern language, you have to be able to hear it in the classroom and the children are not used to being silent for any length of time. This is one of the reasons why teaching modern languages is getting very much more difficult.'

Professor Rée's class included a number of especially difficult children but his experiment must, nevertheless, be typical of what many hundreds of young teachers are facing all over Britain.

The important point is not that discipline in comprehensive schools is often poor and that poor discipline hinders effective teaching. The greater danger is that poor discipline will lead (and is leading) to fundamental changes in the curriculum itself which are justified neither by paedagogic principles nor by national need. Professor Rée believes, perhaps rightly, the French should probably be deferred to the second year of the comprehensive school and that it should be largely voluntary. Because of the great freedom which schools have to determine their own curriculum, it is quite feasible for them to put less emphasis on subjects like modern languages, mainly because they are difficult to teach. Thus, modern studies, environmental projects and the integrated approach to history and geography may gain ascendency because they are more amenable to the style of mixed ability classes, rather than because they are intrinsically superior. Clearly, it is futile to insist that comprehensive schools should teach subjects which cannot be taught. On the other hand, before we accept that the majority of 11 year-olds cannot learn a foreign language, it is worth looking elsewhere.

In Holland, for example, children start to learn English at the age of six. In Sweden, all children are learning two hours of English a week at grade three (age 9) and four hours a week by grade five (age 11). In France, the common curriculum for the first two years of secondary education provides for four hours instruction in a foreign language a week and three hours even for children in the third stream. Even allowing for the fact that national curricula are not implemented successfully in all schools, there is no doubt that the teaching of foreign languages to the majority of pupils is considered, in most of Europe, not only necessary but feasible.

Yet in Britain, the arguments from a considerable body of experts are pointing to the opposite way. Mr. Jim Simpson, Lecturer in Modern Languages at East Anglia University, told a recent symposium (TES 5 March 1976) that the learning of foreign languages should be postponed until the age of 14. He said:

Modern languages, as they are conceived at present, do not fit into any comprehensive education and mixed ability.

He said languages should be taught in intensive courses to gifted minorities — an idea similar to that expressed by Professor Rée. Instead of the conventional approach, most pupils would study the people, culture and places of Europe in a co-operative course designed by geographers, historians as well as linguists. These ides are really a response to the fact that the oral approach which, it was hoped, would replace the traditional methods have, so far, not worked, with the average pupil. And the expensive 'language laboratories', so much in vogue ten years ago, have proved a relative failure. A pupil who is not strongly motivated, soon becomes bored and skips the repetitive exercises.

The teaching of mathematics in secondary schools is labouring under similar difficulties. One cause, already mentioned, is the long-standing shortage of able mathematics teachers. This is linked with the introduction of new courses, of which the School Mathematics Project is perhaps the best known. The course, used in about a fifth of secondary schools, was an attempt to rid the subject of boring repetitive calculations and abstract manipulations. The project tries to introduce the fundamental principles of mathematics, rather than a series of techniques like long division and the manipulation of equations. Children are thus introduced to binary mathematics, topology, set theory and other topics which were previously postponed to advanced studies at 'A' Level or university. This approach is undoubtedly more enjoyable but, unless the teachers are alert, it can lead to the neglect of many of the most basic skills. Science teachers have complained that pupils cannot handle the simple algebraic relations needed in their subjects and employers have found that standards in the functional mathematics required by industry and commerce have fallen.

Recent research by the Coventry and District Employers Federation, indicated a 20 per cent fall in marks gained on a standard test since 1971.

After ten years, the SMP innovators have conceded that more emphasis needs to be put on manipulative skills and practice of examples. Revised courses now include more exercises and a handbook produced by the authors sets out the minimum of mathematical skill required at different ages. However, some teachers, particularly in science departments, still regard the expectations as being unrealistically low. For example, the SMP guide places simple ratio calculations and the whole of algebra beyond the reach of clever 13 year-olds. Average pupils at this age (CSE candidates) are not expected to have great proficiency in the adding, subtraction or division or multiplication of three figure numbers, according to the handbook. On the other hand, these children will have learned, at age 12, that:

$$3 + 3 = 12$$

when the base of four is used for the counting system instead of the base of 10. Without doubt, this fact is mathematically interesting and, in the hands of a good teacher, intellectually stimulating. However, the ability to count and add to the base four is useless in everyday life and work. Such lessons may help towards a deep understanding of numbers, but they may be a positive hindrance to those children who will require practical mathematics in their jobs. The Coventry research seems to indicate that this is happening.

Furthermore, the lowering of standards in simpler manipulative skills is not accidental. It results from a quite explicit clash of curriculum policy between those who wish to emphasize usable skills and those whose main goals are more intellectual and abstract.

When the criticism of SMP maths was put to Dr. Brian Thwaites, Principal of Westfield College, London, and the first director of the project, he stated bluntly that the course was not intended to develop the skills required by industry. He attributes the decline of school maths to poor teaching rather than the effects of his course and points out that the decline had started long before SMP came on the market. He believes that, in the hands of a good teacher, the SMP course can give children plenty of practice in manipulative skills; for although the course books themselves contain very few examples, good teachers will make up their own examples to supplement the books, where necessary.

For Dr. Thwaites, an able mathematician who taught formerly at Winchester, the invention of examples to practice pupils' technique would present no difficulties. Unfortunately, however, many of the teachers who take mathematics classes at present are either not mathematicians at all, poor mathematicians, or inexperienced in the concepts used in the new courses.

Thus, the SMP course is open to a twofold criticism: first that it takes insufficient account of the needs expressed by industry and society at large, for the development of skills in useful mathematics and, secondly, that it has not been framed to give enough help to understaffed schools and harrassed teachers in the school world. It would not be fair to make a total judgement on this maths course only on the basis of the points made so far for it has, in some respects, made valuable improvements: it is more interesting than traditional maths for many pupils and it has won the enthusiastic support of many practising teachers. The present discussion is not intended to evaluate all the pros and cons. It is intended to show first, that the new course has brought fundamental changes in the way the subject is conceived and, in particular, a shift away from the manipulative skills towards a theoretical, intellectual approach; secondly, these changes are controversial, even within the teaching profession. Objections articulated by Mr. Brian Woolnough, Lecturer in the Oxford University Department of Education (TES, 24 January, 1975) centre on the neglect of mathematical skills needed in other school subjects, particularly physics. Thirdly, the changes have been introduced as a result of the efforts of an independent group of teachers and academics in devising the new course and persuading the schools to acept it. The changes were not preceded by any wide discussion of the fundamental issues involved.

The views of industrialists, parents, local authorities and government were not canvassed in any organized way. And although the issues have been debated hotly among professional mathematicians, teachers and educationalists as a whole have been slow to grasp the importance of the policy issues at stake. Fourthly, the new course, though it was clearly experimental, has spread rapidly in secondary schools before the long-term effects could become clear. No public body has had the power to circumscribe the experiment or to prescribe conditions for its evaluation before it was allowed to spread.

None of these four observations is a criticism of the SMP or its originators who have clear aims for which they are prepared to put up a lusty defence. The development of SMP does illustrate, however, the way in which the devolution of curricular decisions to the schools has allowed important decisions of public policy to drift out of public debate and to entirely escape from public control.

This uniquely British lack of system is, moreover, allowing the development of some courses which can, by no means, boast the high level of intellectual thought and careful assembly which, it must be said, went into the production of SMP.

Consider, briefly, the changes taking place in History — a subject which does not have the same obvious relationship to national needs as do maths and foreign languages. Yet, history teaching has, in the past, been seen as important as a way of shaping children's consciousness of national identity and national destiny. It was, no doubt, done in a rather crude and chauvinistic manner by emphasis on the glories of British victories and achievements and contemptuous dismissal of the foreigner. It also dealt mainly with the deeds of heroes and monarchs rather than the sufferings of poor people.

But, whatever the shortcomings of this history, the aims were nevertheless clear and generally agreed, especially in the teaching of younger children. History teachers recounted the great national traditions which, in less advanced societies, have been handed from generation to generation through ballads and folk tales. The stories of Trafalgar, Agincourt and Captain Cook or George Stephenson were, if not propagandist, clearly associated with a general message about courage and enterprise of those who have shaped our institutions and national character. A more critical approach based on evaluation of evidence, motives, bias and conflicting sources was gradually developed amongst older pupils from this base of 'patriotic' history. The exciting stories (Bruce and the Spider, Alfred and the Cakes, 'England expects . . .', the Battle of Britain) were really parables of national excellence.

The emphasis is now shifting rapidly, for several reasons. Firstly, Britain's declining power has made past glories seem less relevant and the histories of other nations more important. Second, the patriotic jingoism which helped to precipitate the First World War, made teachers more sceptical. Thirdly, the over-simplifications of patriotic history have been an easy target for Marxists, cynics and liberal intellectuals. Lastly, the development of project methods and interdisciplinary studies have provided practical ways in which teachers could change the emphasis of history. Some changes have been made in response to profound shifts of ideological perspective. Others have stemmed from the view that history should be made more 'relevant' to working class children who, it is claimed, cannot identify with kings and generals. And these changes have been underpinned by the intellectuals' belief that the subject should introduce even quite young children to historical method rather than just teaching them facts.

Other teachers have just swum with the tide, seldom enquiring about its cause or effects.

Ideally, the project method can broaden children's interest from a particular topic under study to general historical considerations. But too often, children can spend their history periods on a trivial study like 'costume down the ages' which has neither historical stuffing nor a genuine intellectual interest of its own. A guide to the teaching of history, written by practising history teachers (*The Teaching of History in Secondary Schools',* Assistant Masters Association, Cambridge University Press, 1975) says of the project method:

Such learning as does attend the enormous efforts pupils are likely to put into their projects, is often incidental, slipshod and superficial and, if an examination question is asked relating to a pupil's project, it is depressing how frequently it must be of the 'write anything at all you have learned from your project' variety . . . Merely to instruct pupils to do a general project on *fashion,* for instance, and to leave them to get on with it, is to invite regurgitated passages from books and thoughtlessly copied diagrams.

The Masters also condemn the failures which can result from interdisciplinary studies in which history, geography and sociology teachers may combine into a team to teach a general topic like 'The Origins of Civilization'. The Masters say:

> Too often the label (interdisciplinary studies) is attached to
> a course which is less than integrated and frequently less
> than a disciplined study.

They say the less able pupils who are given integrated or 'environmental' studies, lose the 'red-blooded element of history'. Courses designed around the history of their locality often provoke apathy and the Masters say:

> More than one pupil has responded to the grand
> integration scheme with the request: 'Please Sir, can't we
> do proper history, like the others?

The Masters also describe the change of aims of history already discussed:

> In the past, emphasis was on the learning of factual
> information and on the promotion of worthy objectives by
> means such as inculcating national pride, drawing moral
> lessons and providing examples of great men in whose
> footsteps pupils might be urged to tread. Today, concern is
> more with the development of qualities of historical
> imagination, the encouragement of understanding and skills
> and the use of facts to discuss issues rather than ascertain
> right answers.

A similar idea underlay the Schools Council's Humanities Curriculum Project which collected emotive photographs and quotations intended to provoke open discussions on controversial topics like racial prejudice. It was proposed that the teacher should abnegate responsibilities for explicit moral and intellectual guidance and, instead, act as a 'neutral chairman' to regulate orderly debate and try to develop logical thought and discussion.

The liberal dreams that education should improve the minds, stimulate the curiosity and sharpen the reasoning of pupils rather than merely equip them with knowledge and skills has thus become an accepted wisdom amongst curriculum planners. The trouble is that, although the rewards of success are greater, so are the penalties of failure. A child who does a bad project may end up with neither a knowledge of national history nor any worthwhile idea of historical method, beyond copying bits out of the Parish Register and the Encyclopaedia Britannica. The attempt to develop critical minds may, if the children have not assimilated enough data, merely replace patriotism with cynical apathy. This is not a necessary consequence of the new approach but it is a danger which has been too generally neglected. The opposite danger is that teachers who are anxious to broaden pupils' understanding beyond the story of our islands, may try to cram in too much and produce, in the words of the AMA, 'a scamper through the centuries' or 'history of the world from Plato to Nato'. Clearly the best teachers will avoid these extremes and the AMA has, obligingly, described the qualities he should have:

He is, in essence, a temperate man. His enthusiasm is
tempered with realism, his beliefs with doubt. He distrusts
emotional and emotive thinking without discarding warmth
and understanding. He has high principles but knows the
frailty of humanity. His convictions are firm but he
eschews dogmatism. Obsessions, fanaticism, superstition
and prejudice, he abhors. His judgment is sure because it is
based on knowledge. He is not swept away by novelty for
he can distinguish between what is recent and what is new,
between the ephemeral and the lasting. He combines
commitment with objectivity, high standards with
compassion.

No doubt, this splendid neo-Baconian prose describes the qualities of
many practising teachers; under their sage guidance, the reasonably able
pupil must surely prosper, irrespective of the methods and syllabus. But
policy-makers must also consider the effect of changes on the average
teacher, the below average, the minority of idle and incompetent
teachers and the quite large number whose genuine idealism outruns
their ability. It is particularly important to consider the weaker teachers
in relation to new methods and organization, like mixed ability classes,
and new courses, like mixed studies, which often set broader and vaguer
objectives.

Enough has been said to indicate important changes which are taking
place in three subject areas — languages, history and mathematics.
These changes raise four fundamental issues:

1.   The amount of study in each subject — for example, the age at
which French should be started in order to produce the desired
competence.

2.   The balance of subjects required to give a broad general course
appropriate for different ages and abilities.

3.   The curricular objectives of each subject or subject area at different
levels. Recent curriculum developments have so widened the scope of
what is taught that courses under the same label may now almost
constitute different subjects.

4.   The standards which should be aimed at during the courses and the
standards which should be prescribed for successful completion of
them.

VI. Examinations and Standards

Although the British have left most of the curriculum to individual schools and teachers, a fair uniformity of standards has been guaranteed, amongst abler pupils at least, by independent GCE examining boards. Further checks are provided by the national and local inspectorates and, to a very limited extent, by the school governors. The direct influence of the inspectorate on standards has been progressively weakened by the bewildering variety of courses and their diverse aims. New objectives have made the enforcement of standards more debateable as well as more difficult. The outside influence of examinations will also be weakened if current proposals (July 1976) for merging the GCE with the easier Certificate of Secondary Education are adopted. The single examining system for 16-year-olds would, almost certainly, result in a shift of standards towards the average and a coarser discrimination between the abilities of the top 30 per cent of children.

The most important effect would be to put yet more power into the hands of teachers' unions, who would probably control the new examining boards (they already control the 13 regional CSE Boards). Individual teachers would also be given increased scope to devise their own courses and to assess pupils themselves under the 'Mode Three' system already used with the CSE. The desirability of a single system for the examination of the ablest along with the children who are barely literate, is far from established. And the case for making a large addition to the very great freedom enjoyed by teachers has been largely unargued because it has not been seriously opposed.

This is because few people outside education and not many within it, have understood the fundamental long-term changes which the common examination system at 16 could introduce. It is not widely appreciated, for example, that the examinations' function in regulating the curriculum will be much more important in Britain than in other European countries where the curriculum is decided nationally or regionally. Examinations, in short, are a way of keeping a check upon teachers and the curriculum, as well as assessing pupils.

It is essential to bear this caution in mind when considering what may be learned from the practice of examinations in other countries. For example, those who argue that Britain no longer needs an examination at 16-plus on the grounds that there is no outside examination at this age on the continent, overlook the very strict controls over curriculum in the countries they site for comparison.

At the higher level, for potential university students, the difference in practice may be summarized thus:

Britain

The Advanced (A) Level examination is set by the eight GCE Boards, most (but not all) of which are closely connected with universities and reflect the standards which universities require. However, the GCE Boards increasingly reflect the views of practising schoolteachers and many papers have been set to examine new types of course like Nuffield Science. The GCE Boards use a complicated technique of double marking and statistical analysis to ensure that standards between examiners are fair and that year to year variations are minimized. Most research indicates that, within the limitations of this type of examination, the 'A' Level system has a high degree of accuracy and fairness. The system allows the candidate to take anything from one to four or even more subjects. Two passes are the minimum required for university entry but three are necessary for most of the popular courses.

France

The *baccalauréat* differs from 'A' Level in two principal ways. The first is that candidates are obliged to take a range of seven or eight subjects for an overall pass or fail. The options are biased towards science, technology or arts subjects in differing degrees but all include a common trunk. The second difference is in the method of assessment. Baccalauréat scripts are marked by only one examiner but the inherent unreliability of this method is mitigated by a system of oral examinations and consideration of school records by a jury of examiners. In contrast with Britain, the assessment of the candidates' own teachers over the period of the course may influence the award of a certificate.

Germany

The candidates' own teachers play an even more important part in their assessment in Germany. Procedures vary between provinces but the general pattern is for the *Abitur* certificate to be awarded on a combination of marks awarded in three ways: first, assessment by teachers of specified pieces of work in all the eight to ten subjects studied in the sixth form of the *Gymnasium*; second, written examinations in four subjects marked by teachers at the candidates' school and by teachers from another school; thirdly, an oral examination in specified subjects in cases of doubt. This system is fairer to candidates who might perform unexpectedly badly in a written examination but, in comparison with the GCE, it has two defects: it is open to distortion by idiosyncratic policies in a particular school and it results in wide disparities of standard between different parts of the country and between different schools.

Holland

Examinations are set nationally at different levels for the three different types of general secondary school — the grammar schools (*Lyceum*) and the higher and intermediate secondary schools (*HAVO* and *MAVO*). The number of subjects varies from seven for the ablest pupils and five for the less able and the examination is conducted by the schools concerned with outside assessors.

Sweden

Formerly the final examination in the Swedish *Gymnasien* was similar to the *Abitur* but now marks are all awarded by a pupil's teacher on the final year's work with the help of standardized achievement tests. Teachers mark their pupils with grades 1 to 5 but are obliged to put roughly the same proportion of pupils in each grade as would correspond to the 'normal' distribution for the whole of Sweden. Thus the teacher will aim to place the following percentage of his pupils in each grade:

Grade 1	—	7 per cent
Grade 2	—	24 per cent
Grade 3	—	38 per cent
Grade 4	—	24 per cent
Grade 5	—	7 per cent

Exceptions can, of course, be made if a batch of candidates is thought to be well above or well below the average. Head teachers and inspectors help in estimating average performance. It is claimed that this system works reasonably well because Sweden is a relatively homogeneous country. However, the system of assessment by teachers tends to reduce the competitive drive between schools which is promoted by a national examination like the GCE. It may be fairer to pupils who have the misfortune to go to a bad school or have a bad teacher, since the system explicitly tends towards the average. By the same token, an average pupil in an above average class with a good teacher may be penalized since his performance will be measured more relative to his class than to the standards of the nation as a whole. The standardized achievement tests are intended to help overcome the unfairnesses but there are considerable objections to them on the grounds that they do not measure the same things as the assessment of the course actually studied.

This brief review indicates that, whereas the British teacher has greater freedom over the school course, he has less influence than his European counterpart over the assessment of pupils. In practice, however, the courses in Britain are also tightly circumscribed by the examination syllabus which performs a similar function to the national syllabus in other countries.

At a lower level, however, the British teacher has not only greater control over the syllabus but, also, the possibility of designing and marking his own examinations through the CSE Mode 3. This freedom may shortly be extended to encompass the ablest pupils up to the age of 16 and of the less able up to the age of 17, through the proposed Certificate of Extended Education.

It is also clear that the British are unique in allowing sixth formers to specialize to the exclusion of a common core of subjects. Some interesting correlations have been made between the results in different subjects in the *Abitur* and success or relative weakness in university examinations. The results quoted in *Paths to University* (op cit) from P. Orlik, *Kritishe Untersuchungen zur Begabtenförderung* show that success at university is often associated with subjects which a British student would not have studied in the sixth form.

Thus, the best students in medicine score higher in maths but lower in biology than the worst students: the best prediction of success in law appeared to be high scores in music, and geography was negatively correlated with success in arts subjects at university.

Interestingly, the weak students in arts had almost exactly the same examination profile on average as the best students in law. These results indicate that pupils are more flexible than we sometimes assume and that success in a narrow range of 'A' Level subjects may not necessarily be the best predictor of eventual success in a degree in the same, or related, subjects.

Many arguments conspire, therefore, towards the view that British upper sixth form curricula are too narrow. The proposals now being studied by the Schools Council for a two-tier system of Normal and Further Levels to replace the present 'A' Levels, would certainly bring us closer to European practice. Both the French and German systems are moving towards an emphasis on specialist subjects. The proposal for the average university entrant in Britain to study three subsidiary subjects (N Level) and two specialist subjects (F Level) would, therefore, be roughly in line with the emerging pattern in Europe. There are, in any case, independent arguments for compelling, or at least strongly encouraging, all able sixth formers to study one language, English and some combination of science and mathematics up to the age of 18, whatever else they do.

Much of the argument on this question has, so far, been of an educational nature revolving round the conflicts between the need for:
1. A broad general education.
2. High standards and extensive basic knowledge in pre-university specialisms.

3.   Avoiding excessive examination pressure on sixth formers.

This argument will be resolved in the cumbersome committees of the Schools Council by the end of the decade. Meanwhile, it seems pertinent to emphasize several *practical* advantages of a broader curriculum. First, universities and polytechnics would have a better field for recruiting students in unpopular subjects — it may be better for them to take an able student with an 'N' Level in the appropriate subject, rather than a third rate specialist or no student at all. At present, some departments of German are recruiting undergraduate students who have never studied any German before. This fact needs to be set against the claims that intense specialization is essential to maintain university standards. Less specialization would *raise* the standard of entrants to some departments.

Secondly, it seems desirable to insist that all schoolteachers should start their training with a sixth form qualification in Mathematics, English and a language. Only a sharp stipulation of this kind will halt the decline in maths and languages. The rapid reduction of teacher training to match a falling birthrate, provides an opportunity to insist on this minimum and the proposed 'N' and 'F' Levels would provide the means to achieve it. No other European country permits teachers to teach in secondary schools unless they have upper secondary qualifications in these subjects.

Thirdly, industry, commerce and the professions will, increasingly, need people with at least basic numeracy and scientific outlook, as well as competence in foreign languages. More important than this, however, is the general realization throughout Europe that the traditional distinctions between academic and vocational studies are becoming out-dated and self-defeating. As secondary education expanded, courses which were originally conceived for a minority of scholars and their circle of gentlemen have been needlessly extended to many pupils whose future lives will be neither academic nor leisured.

The Swedish Board of Education puts the point succinctly in its introduction to the new integrated upper secondary school:

The distinction between practical and academic education is
and, if the truth were but known, always has been, an
artificial one . . . The physical segregation of the academic
and the practical has produced one-sided groups of pupils
bearing little or no resemblance to the social realities of
subsequent working life.

In Sweden and in France, the governments have tried to respond by instituting technical studies courses in the sixth form. The *baccalauréat de technicien* is still under-prescribed but, in Sweden, some of the ablest pupils are now opting for vocational courses. In Britain, planners have been too late to realize the need to provide such courses in the sixth form, though the Schools Council's *Engineering Science Project* (Macmillan 1974) provides an excellent pointer to what needs to be done to improve the prestige of a subject which, elsewhere, still leads to one of the foremost professions. A broader system of sixth form studies, with three subsidiary and two main subjects, would allow many thousands more pupils to study at least one vocational option without a premature commitment. Efforts will also be needed to ensure that subsidiary options in practical subjects like navigation, cultivation and business management are available to as many sixth formers as want them. Such subjects need not be intellectually inferior to many of the other subjects conventionally designated 'academic'. Even if they prove to be of no direct use in a pupil's subsequent career, they would help him to think constructively and positively about the world of work and gently encourage him to question the inevitability of a blinkered trudge along the academic highroad.

The need to broaden the scope, particularly of sixth form studies, will become particularly acute if a rising proportion of the age group passes GCE 'A' Levels. This is happening in France, Germany and Sweden, which are all educating a steeply rising proportion of children to the upper secondary school level. In France, there is an acute problem of unemployment for many pupils who take the *baccalauréat* but who do not go on to university or drop out after the first year. The severely academic character of most of the sixth form studies does not help students move towards the employment market and efforts are now being made to inject a more vocational element into some of the courses.

A comparison of the numbers gaining the *baccalauréat,* and the German *Abitur* with those obtaining the GCE 'A' Levels indicates, in crude terms, the relative efficiency of the systems in producing academically qualified youngsters.

It is largely a matter of opinion whether the examinations are comparable, since GCE 'A' Level papers are, generally, (but not in all subjects) set at a higher standard than individual papers in the Continental countries. Thus two 'A' Level passes could be taken as the equivalent of the *baccalauréat* and *Abitur* since, together with 5 'O' Levels, they constitute the matriculation requirement for college or university. However, a pupil who has passed only two 'A' Levels may not, in fact, have reached a very high standard. Three 'A' Levels are more usually needed for university entrance and may be a fairer comparison with the upper secondary school leaving examination abroad. Since Britain, France and Germany have approximately the same populations, a crude comparison of gross numbers is possible. The proportions of the age groups passing the examinations are more difficult to establish because of the widespread repetition of grades. Approximate figures only, are given for comparison.

It can be seen from Table 9, that the French school system is very much more efficient than ours in getting children up to the pre-university academic standard, while Germany, which has, in the past, lagged behind, has rapidly overtaken Britain in the last five years. The number passing the *Abitur* has double since 1970. The drive for greater equality has, in Germany, taken the form of encouraging more and more pupils to go to the *Gymnasium* whereas, in Britain, hopes were pinned on the liberalizing effect of comprehensive schools.

Table 9

England and Wales (1973/74)		
Numbers passing GCE 'A' Levels in schools and further education colleges:		
	Number in Thousands	Percentage of leavers
1 or more subjects	132.7	19
2 or more subjects	96.6	14
3 or more subjects	59.8	9
France (1974)		
	Thousands	per cent
Numbers passing the ordinary *baccalauréat*	152.2	
Numbers including technical *baccalauréat*	199.0	
Percentage of age group passing *baccalauréat*		20-25
Germany (1974)		
Number passing *Abitur*	163.3	
(1973)	146.7	
Percentage of age group passing (1973)		16.4

However, the trend of results in Britain has, so far, been disappointing as the following table shows:

Table 10

Percentage of school leavers in England and Wales gaining three or more 'A' Levels	
	Percentage
1963-4	5.5
1968-9	7.8
1971-2	8.2
1973-4	7.9

After a continued rise throughout the 1960s, the success rate is now static or even declining. This pattern is similar to that which emerged from the tests of national reading standards and it is interesting to speculate whether low morale in schools and worsening discipline, changes in courses and teaching methods, or the upheavals of comprehensive reorganization are to blame. It is sometimes suggested that we are approaching a limit because only a certain proportion of children have the natural ability to pass an exam of as high a standard as GCE 'A' Level. Clearly, the proportion of the age group reaching this academic level cannot, even under the most favourable school conditions, increase indefinitely. However, comparisons with Europe give no grounds for the complacent idea that we are giving an academic qualification to all children potentially capable of gaining one. There is good reason to think that the present 'A' Levels offer the wrong sort of course for many capable children who are not interested in an intensive study of two or three narrow academic subjects. However, at this level, intensive study and concentrated coaching must be needed whether the courses are broad, narrow, academic or vocational. There is, therefore, a prima facie case that the British system is simply not delivering the goods as well as the French and German upper secondary schools.

In France, the number passing the technical *baccalauréat* alone is of the same order as the number of passes in three 'A' Levels across the whole subject range in Britain.

Why is it that twice as many French children obtain the *baccalauréat* as are able to get two 'A' Levels in Britain? A large part of the answer must be that French children have to work harder under strong competitive pressure, even from the early primary stage. Excessive competitiveness and pressure clearly have disadvantages particularly for some children who are struggling to keep up. However, the French system with regular gradings, assessments and streaming undoubtedly gets exam results which are, at least, quantitatively much superior to ours. Very similar observations apply to Germany, where the number passing the *Abitur* is already well ahead of the number passing three 'A' Levels in Britain and, increasingly rapidly, at a time when our own 'A' Level successes are stagnating. Demographic and other trends clearly influence the number of exam results, so that too close a comparison would be unfair. But it is, nevertheless, clear that the gap between British and Continental performance is very substantial and it is widening.

This is not to say that Britain should be stampeded to adopt the teaching and examination methods of European competitors, for it remains true that, at best, the 'A' Level courses offer greater scope for genuine intellectual development, while the more relaxed atmosphere in our system gives pupils a better chance of developing true interest in their subject. Enthusiasm is often destroyed by the competitive treadmill of the French and Germany systems. Indeed, the thoroughgoing reforms brought forward by the French Education Minister, M. Haby, were aimed to liberalize the sixth forms by deferring selection to the *lycée* stream until after 15 or 16. On the other hand, British educationists should urgently consider whether the habits of discipline and the effects of competition of French and German children may not have an important effect on their later habits of work, not only in the sixth forms, but in industry and commerce. In other words, a system which is more efficient in producing exam results may also be more efficient at producing motor cars and other exports. And a system which concentrates too much on personal development and academic enlightenment may produce a people which is more relaxed, less highly stressed, subtler and poorer.

Standards

Direct comparisons of examination results is open to several criticisms. First, that the systems are not comparable. Secondly, that schools and pupils have wider objectives than cramming for exams. Thirdly, some progressive teachers even question the usefulness of external standards, saying that intellectual growth is fundamentally a personal matter. However, efforts have been made to compare international standards through an impressive series of standardized tests devised by the International Association for the Evaluation of Educational Achievement (IEA) in Stockholm. Results at sixth form level are inconclusive because of the different rates of selection for sixth form classes. Clearly, average sixth form standards in mathematics in a country like the USA, where 75 per cent of the pupils stay on at school, are likely to be lower than average sixth form standards in Britain where only the cleverest follow the course. When standards of the ablest pupils are compared it is found, predictably perhaps, that there is not very much difference between countries. However, the Institute has found that the factors which influence standards in mathematics most are 'time given to instruction in mathematics' and 'time given to mathematics homework'. At age 14, when most children are still doing compulsory time-tabled mathematics, the amount of homework was the most influential factor. This point is well-worth emphasizing at a time when the whole idea of homework in British schools in coming into question. A report on the subject by the Assistant MistressesAssociation (1974) discussed the difficulties of setting homework in modern mixed ability schools and suggested that the practice should become less frequent.

The IEA science survey *(Science in 19 countries,* 1973) contains the following interesting information in tabular form:

Table 11

Homework undertaken by children			
	11 year olds Hours home-work per week	Per cent who have no homework	14 year olds Hours home-work per week
England	1	60	5
Netherlands	7	27	8
Germany	7	3	8
Sweden	3	8	4
Japan	7	2	7

It is clear that British children below the sixth form level are required to do less homework and the proportion which does no homework at all is greater than in most other European countries. It should be remembered, however, that German schools close at lunchtime so that there is more time, as well as perhaps more need, for homework. The amount of homework amongst pre-university pupils in the sixth form is broadly comparable between the countries.

The survey also indicates that, in science at least, British teachers have had shorter training and spend less time per week on preparation.

Table 12

Science Teachers				
	11 year-olds		**Sixth formers**	
	Average training of teachers in years	Hours spent in preparation per week	Hours of preparation	Percentage of teachers with university training
England	2.3	4.9	6.2	67
France	not available		10.4	92
Germany	3.6	9.8	13.5	98
Netherlands	3.3	5.1	7.3	87
Sweden	2.1	6.9	12.2	98

The average standard of English 14 year-olds in science was about comparable with that in Sweden and the USA, better than in Holland but well below the standard in Japan and Hungary. It is worth noting that Japan and Hungary are both characterized by a highly disciplined and formal approach to teaching with an emphasis on rote learning. The standard deviation indicates the range between the best and worst

Table 13

Mean Science scores and standard deviation amongst 14 year-old pupils		
	Mean Score	Standard Deviation
Japan	31.2	14.8
England	21.3	14.1
Sweden	21.7	11.7
Germany	23.7	11.5
Netherlands	17.8	10.0
USA	21.5	11.6
Hungary	29.1	12.7

pupils which is higher in England than in any of the other European countries. The high standard deviation in Japan, probably measures the casualty rate amongst those who cannot keep up with the forced regimental pace. Unfortunately, England suffers nearly the same casualty rate without achieving the same average high standard.

The differences shown in Table 13 are not dramatic and are, in any case, hard to interpret because of different national approaches. However, substantially less time spent by British teachers and pupils in preparation helps to explain the relatively small numbers reaching GCE 'A' Level compared with the equivalent levels in France, Germany and Sweden.

One further point which emerges with striking clarity from the IEA survey, is the gulf between science and literature in the sixth forms, which is very much more marked in England than elsewhere.

At junior school level, the correlation between ability in science and in reading is high in all countries. But, in the sixth form, the survey shows what the IEA report calls a 'dramatic documentation' of the 'two cultures' phenomenon in Britain. In Swedish and American schools, the sixth-form correlation between science and English comprehension has dropped to about 0.6 (correlation of 1.0 is a perfect match correlation of 0 means no relationship at all). But in a comparison of English schools, the correlation was only 0.16. When the relationship between science and literature was studied, it was found that the correlation was actually negative. This means that the schools which do well in science, do badly in literature and vice versa. It is quite clear from the survey that this is a peculiar result of the British school system and, by no means, a necessary fact about pupils.

Summary and Suggestions

A strong case can, therefore, be made out that Britain is out of line with Europe and, indeed, with the rest of the world, in allowing pupils to specialize to the exclusion of the basic common core subjects. It has not been sufficiently realised that the comparison between British sixth formers taking three 'A' Levels and possibly two non-examinable options and the French *baccalauréat* student is unrealistic. Increasing numbers of English students are now taking 'A' Levels in ones and twos. Even if those only obtaining one pass are included, the total number of pupils obtaining 'A' Levels is substantially below the number obtaining the *baccalauréat*.

Furthermore, narrow specialization emphasises academic rather than vocational values at a time when most European countries are realising the need to make upper secondary studies point towards the world of work as well as to the rarified domain of university and college.

No comparative arguments can be conclusive because the general emphasis of school curricula depends on the consensus in society about the general aims for which schools should be striving.

In Britain, no attempt has been made to formulate such a consensus amongst citizens as a whole. And even within the teaching profession, decision-making is much more fragmented than elsewhere. Individual head teachers may not have much idea of national needs. Even where they have, their decisions may cancel out, for heads have neither the time nor the necessary information to arrive at an overall perspective.

The Schools Council, set up by the government in 1964, to consider broad questions of curriculum and examinations, suffers from several crippling limitations and defects:

1. It is controlled by representatives of the teachers' unions, particularly the National Union of Teachers, whose representatives are often officials rather than teachers and, in many cases, well removed from the practice of the classroom.

2. Representation of industry, the universities, the professions and society at large, is very small. (The CBI and the TUC have only one representative each out of the 74 members of the governing council).

3. The Council has now powers over what happens in schools and the recent emphasis of 'Dissemination and in-service training' (December 1974) is evidence of concern that projects are being ignored by schools.

4. The Council has developed a bureaucracy and committee structure of Byzantine complexity, which has effectively prevented worthwhile debate on many of the major issues. Caucus politics has taken over, with the inevitable result that the general leftist teacher-orientated line of the National Union of Teachers has prevailed.

5. Nearly all the important debates of the Council's proliferating committees are held in private. Discussion by a wider public has therefore been truncated.

The Schools Council is a peculiarly British response to the fear of allowing political control over the curriculum. This fear is often associated with appeals to principles of freedom and warnings of what could happen to our school courses if a tyrant were in control. In reality, however, teachers' influence has, like much else in the British system 'just grown'. Because teachers have stridently defended their stockade, the public has been slow to recognize what is clearly understood in most other countries — that many issues about school curricula are of a profoundly political nature. What is taught to children, inevitably reflects as well as moulds society.

Methods are needed, therefore, for public discussion and control of curricula and examinations. A standing national commission has been proposed with representation from a wide range of interests. This could be successful, provided a way could be found of articulating opinions from outside the teaching profession.

At the same time, policy makers must ask whether the national government should not play a more direct part in determining what is taught in the schools for which the Minister has overall responsibility. Parliamentary democracy, with all its defects, is the method by which we determine important issues of national policy in all other spheres. So why not in schools? If the government were to take a more direct initiative over, for example, the future of GCE 'A' Levels, the result could well be a wider public discussion of the issues. The present introverted procedure of the Schools Council, besides being inordinately slow, has given most outsiders the false idea that the decisions are 'entirely educational' and, therefore, nothing to do with them. After more than ten years of discussion within the Schools Council, the government will be presented with a proposal which it can either approve or reject but will have the greatest difficulty in varying.

The broad issues of curriculum policy do not need ten years of discussion. They could easily be defined in as many weeks. The government should then publish a discussion paper on the central policy issue, after which wide public discussion could precede a decision in principle. The detailed curricula should, logically, follow such a decision and not precede it as at present. The procedure by which the Schools Council commissions detailed 'feasability studies' in advance of a national decision is like asking engineers to study the nuts and bolts needed for a new car before the overall design has been settled.

An advisory committee on standards and course design would provide a means by which the Minister could be alerted to the major issues requiring national debate and of additional powers which he may need to take. It should differ from the Schools Council, not merely in being more representative, but in being directly responsible to the Minister (whereas the Schools Council has become responsible to no-one). Revolutionary as this idea may appear, it would represent only the most cautious and conservative move towards the kind of public control accepted throughout Europe. Most Europeans must smile to see that a British Secretary for Education, who is seriously concerned about mathematics standards in schools, is reduced to public exhortation from a conference platform (Mr. Fred Mulley, North of England Conference, Lancaster, January 1976) rather than effective direct action from his ministry office.

Before concluding this chapter, it is worth disposing of several false objections which will be made against any proposal to increase governmental control or influence over school courses.

That it is inconsistent with principles of a free market in education.

This argument fails because we do not have a free market. Independent schools would be exempt from all but the most general controls. Parents opting for the maintained system already have little choice, and are likely to have even less as the schools become larger and more homogeneous. A free market choice could only work if parents had much greater power to choose schools and, therefore, to reject those whose curricula and ideology they did not like.

That Government control of curricula matters would repress the initiative of practising teachers.

Such fears are founded on the illusion that central control needs to be an all-or-nothing affair. Limited guidelines and general policies need not be as stringent as those in centralist France or Sweden. Most of the design and running of courses could still be left largely to teachers.

Constraints upon them need not, necessarily, be stronger than those formerly exerted by the inspectors.

That control of the syllabus has been abused by tyrants.

By the time a tyrant starts interfering with school courses, the battle for freedom has been lost anyway. The administrative complexity of our system would be unlikely to defeat a determined dictator. The safeguard against such abuses is a democratic Parliament. The alternative of ceding all control to the schools has delivered many children to the tyranny of fashion.

VII. Parents and Teachers – Ideologies and Attitudes

It has long been known that the opinions and interests of parents are among the most important influences on a child's progress at school. Consequently, children of average ability from educated homes often do better than cleverer children from poor families. This cliché of educational theory is being given new emphasis in the proportion of schools which, after comprehensive reorganisation, serve a restricted neighbourhood. Increasingly, teachers are relating their failures and problems to the home background of pupils. Sometimes, it is a way of passing the buck, of finding excuses. But the enormous importance of parental support has been confirmed by research as well as by the experience of teachers (Jencks' *Inequality* (op cit) and the reports of *Educational Priority* Vols 2 and 3, are among the most important).

Clearly, parents who tolerate dishonesty, indiscipline, swearing and idleness cannot reasonably expect schools to remedy all their neglect. On the other hand, such parents, though they often produce children who are a menace to society and to orderly schooling, are happily in a minority, although it is a minority which wastes an inordinate amount of schools' time and energy. This has sometimes diverted teachers from the importance of carrying the support of the majority of decent parents with solid, if unspectacular, ambitions for their children. There are three other trends which threaten to widen the gulf between parents and teachers. The first is the increasing concentration of feckless parents in deprived city areas (though deprived parents are by no means always feckless). Second is the antagonism from the middle classes to what they believe are sloppy and ineffective methods. The third is the bewilderment of many working people about the complexity of new teaching, the patronizing jargon of educationists, the diversity of aims and, above all, the discrepancy between the grandiose things teachers say they are doing and what often appears to be happening in the classroom.

For many parents, the school system appears like Kafka's Castle — full of helpful people, who know all the answers except the one which matters and can pass a parent onto similarly "helpful" people. So, a parent who asks the forbidden question: 'How can I make them teach my son mathematics properly?' will, if he persists, be given a kindly exposition of why the school is *not* doing it. If he is still unsatisfied, he will be passed politely to some, but not all, of the following:

the head teacher, a school councillor, a manager, the chairman of the managers, the deputy divisional officer, the education psychologist, the local inspector, the local councillor, the chairman of the education committee, Her Majesty's Inspector, an M.P., the Minister of Education.

Every one of these individuals shares the responsibility for answering the parents' question and, in specified circumstances, has power to act. Small wonder then, that many parents do not ask simple questions which provide complicated answers.

If teachers are to gain more support from parents, these conditions are necessary:

1. A method of contact, like a parent-teacher association.
2. Parents must understand what the school is trying to do and how it aims to do it.
3. The parents' ideas about the purpose of schooling and their general ideology must be reasonably in tune with those of the teachers. Middle class, conservative parents will not support extreme left or progressive teachers; nor should they be expected to do so without a great deal of persuasion.

In Britain the lack of agreed curricula and the great mixture of methods make good contact between parents and teachers even more important than in most other countries. However, the IEA science survey (op cit) showed that parent-teacher associations are much less common in Britain than elsewhere.

Parent-teacher associations are obligatory in most countries (including France) at the secondary stage and are usual in the primary schools. The low figure on the Netherlands (see Table 14) is balanced by a high degree of parent participation resulting from the private ownership of the schools, supported by the Government.

Clearly, parent-teacher associations do not, themselves, guarantee good contacts between the home and the school. In some schools, associations are moribund, in others, they are dominated by a small minority of the pushy middle classes and, in yet others, relations with parents thrive in spite of the absence of any formal association.

On the other hand, teachers' resistance to formal links with parents have often been for bad reasons. Either they are unwilling to have their methods scrutinized or they are too lazy to run associations. Even where associations exist, teachers usually see them as a way of 'educating' parents rather than for two-sided discussions about what school should be for.

The need for such discussions was amply demonstrated by the Schools Council Enquiry mentioned in the introduction. More recent studies

Table 14

Percentage of schools with Parent-Teacher Associations		
	Primary	Lower Secondary (age 14)
England	40	48
Germany	97	94
Japan	99	100
Netherlands	77	28
Sweden	75	98

indicate that the conflict between the teachers' and parents' ideas of the purpose of schooling is as great as ever. In a detailed survey of three comprehensive schools (*Parents and Teachers,* Schools Council, Macmillan 1976) James Lynch and John Pimlott found that two-thirds of parents wanted more more say over the curriculum and teaching methods. They wanted this even though they were not, on the whole, dissatisfied with the schools and they did not necessarily want to be represented on governing bodies.

The authors say:

> There were highly significant divergences of opinion amongst teachers and parents on the extent to which it was felt that parents had sufficient say in the school and these divergencies were not related to parental satisfaction or dissatisfaction with the school. From this, and the broader evidence or development elsewhere, it seems safe to say that the former cosy consensus between parents and teachers is, gradually, changing. The implications of such a development are clear, in terms of a renegotiation of the contractual relationship between parents and the professional, political, lay and administrative people at present in control of our schools.

The authors also describe the 'somewhat alarming' opinion of roughly three out of four teachers that they were capable of teaching without the parents' help and the fact that the majority of the teachers thought that the parents had enough to say on what and how their children should be taught. The survey confirms the finding of Schools Council Enquiry No. 1 that the parents of 15 year-olds were considerably more interested in standards of discipline, reading, writing, arithmetic and speech than were the teachers, who stressed developments of personality and character.

Lynch and Pimlott say:

> By far the larger number of parents felt that the teaching of reading, writing and arithmetic was very important and other vocationally-orientated skills were, on the whole, highly scored by the parents. Non-vocational aims were rated less highly.

The authors suggest that more effort should be made to allow parents into classrooms and to promote visits to parents' homes by teachers.

A very similar pattern emerges from another recent study of teachers' attitudes to primary school work *(The Aims of Primary School Education: a study of Teachers' opinions,* Patricia Ashton, Pat Keen, Frances Davies and B. J. Holley, Schools Council, 1975).

In a survey of 1,500 teachers in more than 200 schools, 72 aims were ranked in order of importance. The aim given top priority by teachers was that the children should be 'happy, cheerful and well-balanced'. The aims given top ratings showed a strong bias towards personal and moral virtues, for example, 'courtesy and good manners' (No. 8). The teaching of definable skills was, by contrast, often given a relatively low priority by the teachers. Thus, 'everyday maths' ranked only 15th, well below 'enjoyment of school work', 'tolerance' and 'enthusiastic and eager'. The 'four rules of arithmetic' ranked only 20th, while 'correct spelling' came 33rd, 'write clear and meaningful English' came 44th, far below 'enjoyment of leisure interests' which came 18th. Games, gym and body control were all ranked amongst the least important. 'Understanding of modern technology' came sixth from bottom of the list. 'Simple science' came 11th from bottom. Enjoyment of music and skill for simple music making came 7th and 8th from bottom and learning a foreign language was rated least important of 72 aims.

This list is a fairly devastating indictment of the slack and sentimental attitudes which now pervade our primary schools. The teachers' order of priorities was reflected closely in the opinions of secondary school teachers, except that they put rather more emphasis on the skills of reading, writing and arithmetic. Tutors at teacher training colleges also showed the same pattern of priorities. The study identified two main types of teachers: the 'societal' teachers with broadly traditional aims and an emphasis on the three 'Rs' and the 'individualistic' teachers who had more progressive aims like developing reasoned judgements. There are differences in the kind of children the two types of teachers want to produce.

The societal teachers want children to know the moral values shared by the majority of society and to be beginning to acquire the values on which to base their own behaviour. More than this, they want them to know the rules of acceptable social conduct. They think they should be courteous and well mannered and know how to behave appropriately in a wide variety of social situations, be careful and respectful of property and obedient. In quite marked contrast with this wish for the child to conform to external accepted standards, the individualistic teachers want, above all, that children should feel self-confident and personally adequate. They want him to be happy, cheerful, well balanced, enthusiastic and eager, adaptable and flexible.

Here, in the cautious language of research, is a clear documentation of the wild lurches of fashion which have beset some teachers and schools. In this connection, it is highly significant that the study found that those who were the most progressive tended to be younger, less experienced teachers who had spent a short time in their present school — teachers without experience of outside teaching. By contrast, the more traditional teachers were older, more experienced, had spent longer in their present school and were married.

This survey shows three things of great importance. First, it shows the dissension in the teaching profession itself about what the objectives of schools should be. Secondly, it shows a dangerous confusion between aims and means. For example, 'enjoyment in school work' may help children to learn effectively but it does not guarantee that they will do so. Furthermore, if enjoyment is promoted as one of the most important aims, teachers are in danger of rejecting important parts of learning like correct spelling and arithmetic practice, merely because they cannot contrive to make them enjoyable. This is a sentimental perversion of progressive theories which claim merely to have found more enoyable ways of learning spelling and arithmetic. They have not been sold to parents as substituting enjoyment as the end product of schooling.

The third point to emerge from this survey is the penchant of teachers to emphasize vague general goals which are difficult to define, whose promotion in the hurly-burly of the classroom must be very uncertain and whose success is impossible to measure.

Thus, everyone would agree that it is desirable for children to be 'happy. cheerful and well-balanced' to be 'tolerant' and to show 'individuality' and it is obvious that teachers should strive to promote these qualities. But is it right that they should be elevated as the major aims of schooling at the expense of the more definable, if lowlier, attainments in literacy, numeracy, the arts, crafts and music? Inevitably, teachers will fail to make all children happy and tolerant. Indeed, there are powerful arguments to suggest that teachers have little influence over such qualities compared with parents and the home circumstances. On the other hand, the learning of skills is a task in which almost no child need fail altogether. There can be scarcely any doubt that most parents will rate the practical and the measurable outcomes of schooling highest. And it argues an arrogance among teachers who ignore or reject the clear indications of what parents want. Above all, the education service needs a much greater realization of the values which, irrespective of pedagogic or personal advantage, are of paramount importance to the survival and prosperity of a small trading nation. Perhaps, as a civilized society, we can justify giving top priority to making children 'happy and cheerful' at school, but it is, surely, the wildest folly to allow teachers to relegate the aim of producing 'industrious, persistent and conscientious' pupils to the 36th place on their list, lower than being 'a good social mixer'. Are we not in danger of suggesting to our children that happiness is quite separate from, or even incompatible with hard work? It may be argued that because diversity is an advantage, teachers must be allowed to work out their own aims and methods. It is suggested they can only teach with conviction what they believe in. Both these arguments have some substance but they are currently over-rated. Teachers are not philosopher kings, and there must be many capable of doing a reasonably good job in the classroom who have neither the time, the inclination nor the ability to sit down and work out from first principles the purpose of society and their schools' relationship to it. Moreover, there is a danger that teachers will formulate aims which reflect their own weaknesses. At a time when over 40 per cent of those entering colleges of education have not passed GCE 'O' Level mathematics, this may have serious consequences.

Possibly, the British would recoil from a national statement of school aims as detailed and as comprehensive as that published by the Swedish government in Lgr 69. The general section alone, on the principles and aims of compulsory education runs to over 100 pages, with eleven separate documents for the compulsory subjects and a further 16 guidelines for optional and general subjects. Nevertheless, Lgr 69 does state clearly what society expects of schools. It is informed, throughout with an unambiguous vision of the ideal of social democratic society. It states:

The school is part of the community. If it is to succeed in
helping pupils to become good members of the community,
then it must impart a knowledge of the community and
strengthen their sense of belonging to society.'

Even policy statements of this very general sort may be necessary at a time when consensus is breaking up. However, Lgr 69 goes on to show in some detail how the aims should be realized in practice. It stresses the importance of good contacts with parents, suggests ways ' organizing class meetings for parents to discuss topics of general interest with the teacher. It outlines the organization of pupils' councils and staff meetings, the leisure pursuits of pupils as well as the organization and methods of school work. The Swedish view is that certain values and aims are decided by a democratic Parliament and it is the duty of teachers, whatever their personal pursuasions, to adhere to them. On other topics, the teacher is enjoined to remain as fair and objective as possible. In Britain, a common consensus of ideals still exists and probably embraces most schools but, because it is unwritten and often implicit, it relates to general moral objectives rather than to fitting children into society. Thus of the 72 objectives identified in *Aims of Primary Education, not one* refers to fitting children to be future citizens of Britain. Patriotism, democracy, industry, society or community are words which are not mentioned in the teachers' catalogue of objectives and, indeed, they have an alien ring.

The reason is that British teachers have won and held their pedagogic freedom by eschewing all political goals.

It is an unwritten pledge which, in contrast with European practice, attempts to resolve political conflict about aims by pretending that conflict cannot exist. 'If the politicians leave us alone, we will avoid politics' they say. However, this very stand of neutrality is misleading

whilst new techniques, new courses and new types of school
are being developed at an unprecedented rate. In France or Germany,
where teachers are civil servants, a more formal relationship exists
between the aims set out by the government and the individual beliefs
of those who are paid to implement them. however, difficulties must
arise in any free society with the minority of teachers which is
fundamentally opposed to the society which they are employed to serve.
The growth of extreme revolutionary Marxism has been based, in
Britain, on a few universities and polytechnics of which Essex and the
North London Polytechnic are the best known. The students who
erupted into public consciousness during the riots of 1968 are now
becoming established as teachers. Some of their extremes of
revolutionary fervour have, doubtless, been mellowed by promotion but
there can be little doubt that the staff rooms of schools and colleges
have seen a substantial shift towards radicalism in the past few years.

The danger of this process is not that the revolutionary cells will grow
in strength until they overthrow society. The nasty spectacles of
thuggery, intimidation and intolerance abetted and even dignified by the
excessive liberality of academics, has now sufficiently shocked the
public and the educational establishment to prevent a further slide. The
danger is rather that partly by seepage and partly by explicit
compromise, the radical prejudices against authority, discipline and the
production of wealth will further infect the educational consensus.
These ideas can be particularly destructive of society when they are
absorbed by emotional osmosis into the philosophy of liberals who have
neither the informing vision of Marxism nor, on the other hand, a
rigorous understanding of the practical demands of a market economy.
A remarkably frank exposition of the Marxist viewpoint was published
recently by Mr. Maurice Levitas, Senior Lecturer at Neville's Cross
College of Education, Durham *(Marxist perspectives in the Sociology of
Education,* Routledge & Keegan Paul, 1974). To him, victory in the
class struggle and the promotion of social revolution are of paramount
importance. Selection, streaming of children by ability, selection for
training and fostering of personal ambitions are all seen as favouring
the upper class and, therefore, need to be modified or rejected. And
although he rejects the Midwinter formula (ibid) of diluting the
academic content of schooling in order to give a leg up to the working
classes it is difficult to see how his prescriptions can avoid this
outcome, for he cannot explain how the highest intellectual disciplines
leading, for example, to science, medicine or engineering can be taught
without selection of able pupils.

Mr. Levitas' outlook can be summarized in this quotation:

Such class consciousness must carry with it the will and
action to break the power of a now socially valueless
capitalist class.Its progressive elimination as a class can
then run simultaneously with the introduction of a socialist
system of society . . . A hierarchy of occupational statuses
will thus be rendered obsolescent and education will be free
to develop in the new recruits to society their latent

intellectual aesthetic moral and physical power without
reference to positions of dominance or subordination in
society.

The absurdity of using such visionary clichés as a basis for the training
of teachers in present-day Britain does not need to be demonstrated.
However, it is worth considering the practical method of introducing
the class struggle into comprehensive schools, which Mr Levitas seeks to
promote.

Three avenues seem to be immediately open:
i)   the representation of working class organisations on
governing bodies.
ii)   progress in the development of the class consciousness
of teachers — that is, of their perception of themselves as
the teaching proletariat.
iii)   growth of pupils' or students' unions. And the most
important element in that class consciousness would seem to
be, in respect of education, the awareness that systems of
selection *as well as drives for upward mobility* (author's
itals) serve those who wish to use the schools mainly for the
provision of a differentiated labour force.

Alas, in that brief period before the millenium, the production of an
undifferentiated labour force, together with other measures which Mr
Levitas recommends, will produce economic stagnation and decline.
Indeed, it seems that they are already beginning to do so.

There follows a question which it is fashionable to avoid asking:
'Should Mr Levitas and people with similar views be allowed to train
our future teachers?'

Clearly, the freedom to hold subversive views must be granted by a
free society but should we actually pay people to propagate them?
Atheists are not eligible to be priests, nor may Catholics become heads
of Quaker Schools. Can we make a similar distinction between those
who want to preserve, improve or reform our present society and those
who want to destroy it? Can we define an absolute distinction between
those who campaign for change and those who agitate for revolution?

Unfortunately, such distinctions are seldom clear in practice.
Philosophical objections are immediately raised as well as the spectre of
a hysterical witch-hunt, whose consequences would be repugnant to the
democratic ideal. Those who think glibly of sacking a few Marxists
'pour encourager les autres' tend to forget that intolerance is double-
edged.

Nevertheless, the problem of where the limits of tolerance should be
drawn in the education systems of free societies is serious, as can be
seen from the current purge of Marxist teachers from schools,
universities and colleges in Germany. The purge stems from a Federal
decree in January 1972, banning extremists from employment in the
Civil Service. The decree was a reaction to the violent disturbances in
the universities in 1968 and the Marxist take-over of several institutions,
notably the Free University of Berlin. The decree stated that
membership of an organization which conflicted with the constitution
of the Federal Republic should be taken to be enough evidence that the

person was unsuitable for employment in the Civil Service By January, 1975 is was reported (Guardian, 14 January, 1975) that at least 300 people, including one professor, had been rejected from teaching posts or were refused the renewal of their contracts on political grounds. An attempt has been made to impose uniform criteria for screening applicants in all the 11 provinces. A Bill specifying the details was passed by the *Bundestag* in October 1975, but it was rejected in the Upper House. The decree met strong objection in principle. It has also operated most crudely so that, even by their own criteria, the authorities have sometimes got the wrong people and missed others who were more extreme. Some teachers it is said, have been condemned because of friendships made years back in university days, whilst others have not been touched because they wield political influence through the trade union movement. The decree also opens the door to the squalid operations of informers and campus police and the paying off of professional scores. Yet, in spite of widespread resentment amongst liberals and left wingers, the decree has exercized a steadying influence on the system. Students have shown much greater reluctance to join left-wing disruptions and teachers have been much more cautious about left-wing influences.

The acceptance of the *Berufsverbot* has been made easier by the fact that, as in France, German teachers are civil servants and, therefore, are accustomed to a stricter discipline than in Britain. They are, for example, allocated to posts instead of applying for them, as in Britain. They can be moved from one post to another, whereas British teachers cannot generally be moved to another school. As a result, the regional and central bureaucracies have much more influence on promotion prospects of French and German teachers. In Britain, by contrast, promotion is still very much an individual matter between a teacher and his headmaster or governors. Consequently, the pressure to conform to accepted values is considerably greater in France and Germany, even without a decree against extremists. In Holland, the safeguards are different, since so many of the schools are in private hands and teachers are, inevitably selected according to the general outlook of particular governors, as happens in the private sector in Britain. In this case, broad conformity with the owners' own philosophy of education is an obligation on the teacher — even if an unspoken one.

The stated opinions of teachers may be less important in the long run, than their quality. For parents will tolerate teachers with whom they disagree if they are good enough. Indeed, the greatest difficulty of applying research techniques to education is that almost any teaching method (or no method at all) can get good results in the hands of an able teacher — and with suitable children. Thus, the total freedom practiced by A. S. Neill at Summerhill worked because Neill was a great teacher, but many people who tried to imitate Neill, particularly in the USA, failed miserably, as he sadly records in his autobiography. *Neill! Neill! Orange Peel!* (Hart, 1972).

Present day education in Britain is littered with similar failures of teachers who tried to imitate the famous innovators but found, after reading the books and going to the lectures, that their own competence and industry simply was not up to the task. The crucial importance of improving the quality of teachers was recognized in the two major reports of the 1970s: the James report on Teacher Training and in the Bullock Report on Reading. Both advocated a substantial increase in the amount of 'in-service training' or retraining of teachers. 'In-service-training' has thus been regarded as something of a panacea for improving the quality of teaching, partly because it is the only measure on which politicians, administrators and all the teachers' unions could easily agree. However, in the absence of general agreement about aims and methods of teaching, retraining of teachers will not necessarily achieve much improvement. The danger is that many retraining courses will be concerned with the dissemination of novelty and 'exciting ideas' which almost always demand harder work and greater skill from the teachers.

The highly skilled and hardworking teachers are probably experimenting anyway. They do not need retraining. Others may be given new ideas without the skills needed for their implementation. The most important reform, therefore, would be to improve the calibre of those entering the profession. The barrier of low pay has been largely removed by the 30 per cent upgrading following the Houghton Report (January 1975) while the declining demand for teachers should allow schools to be more selective. One of the present difficulties, is that the rapid expansion of the 1960s, obliged colleges to accept — and to pass — very many students with poor qualifications. In spite of hopes for an improvement, applications for 1975/76, for initial training, were 5,300 (or ten per cent) lower than in the previous year. Reports of a reduction in the demand for teachers may be partly responsible but, it is also likely that the increasing worries about discipline and academic standards in schools are depressing recruitment. Of the 43,000 applications, 11,200 withdrew and a further 1,500 were unqualified. This left 31,000 applicants for 29,600 places.

In other words, almost anyone with the minimal educational qualifications can train to be a teacher in Britain. Only 30 per cent had two or more GCE 'A' Levels. A quarter of those accepted had only reached GCE 'O' Level standard and nearly nine per cent had only the minimum of five 'O' Levels. Of all the students accepted for training, 41 per cent had not been able to pass 'O' Level mathematics. Of the 'A' Levels passed by qualified candidates, only 1,230 or 3.5 per cent of all the subjects passed were in mathematics, compared with 24 per cent in the other key subject of English literature and 10 per cent in geography. No rational argument can justify the recruitment of seven times as many aspiring teachers with 'A' Levels in English literature and nearly three times as many qualified in a minor subject like geography, compared with those with passes in mathematics.

The position of science is scarcely more encouraging. Only 473 men and women students were recruited who passed physics at 'A' Level.

This represents about one teacher for every ten secondary schools and less than one for every 60 schools overall. The number of qualified in chemistry is almost exactly the same, whilst the combined number in metalwork, woodwork and technical drawing was only 514. *(Annual Report Central Register and Clearing House Limited — Autumn 1975 Entry).*

Although colleges may try to remedy these omissions, there can be little confidence that all the students emerging from teacher training colleges will have achieved a desirable balance of studies. Mr. Charles Fox, Lecturer in Physical Science at Middleton St. George College of Education, Darlington, estimated (TES 20.20.76) that only one fortieth of the average students' studies was devoted to science in the curriculum. This represents a reduction from 1/26th of time spent on science when the college opened in 1968. The reduction in time spent studying the teaching of science was a direct result of a reorganization into two subject areas called 'environmental studies' and 'aesthetic studies'.

The inadequacy of science and mathematics training in colleges of education is particularly serious at a time when efforts are being made to introduce science courses developed by the Nuffield Foundation in to the primary school. However good the courses, they will not succeed unless the teachers, themselves, have an adequate grounding in the subject. Indeed, the Nuffield Science Project 5/13 is already showing the same symptoms of asphyxiation which have killed off the primary school French project (its demise was mentioned earlier).

Mr. Fox writes with the despairing resignation of many who see their subjects threatened with disuse:

> There is little we alone can do since, in a democratic society, the wishes of the majority are usually allowed to prevail. All we can do is to make the facts plain, whenever we are given the opportunity and make them available to whoever might like to notice them.

So great is the prejudice in Britain against forcing pupils and students to study subjects they think they will not like, that many people have failed to notice such facts or to appreciate their significance. Professor Sir Hermann Bondi, Chief Scientific Adviser to the Ministry of Defence, has identified one reason:

> The negative attitude to mathematics, unhappily so common even among otherwise educated people, is surely the greatest measure of our failure and is a real danger to our society. Not everyone can (or should) be a great mathematician but, surely, the attitude to mathematics should be the same as to other subjects — namely, that anyone who wants to acquire reasonable competence can do so. No-one claims that special aptitude is needed to become moderately good at Dutch or even at Chinese, at Greek, history or golf; all you need is a willingness to work at it. I have no doubt that mathematics ought to be in the same category. But for many, it is not. (TES, 26 March 1976)

The unpopularity of sciences and mathematics and the low status of teacher training for primary schools is something which most non-Communist countries have had to face in varying degrees; but Britain has had greater difficulties for two reasons:

The first is the large amount of choice given to individual students in the studies they will pursue. They may, for example, take anything from one to nine 'O' Levels spread over a period of two to three years. In France, Germany, Sweden or Holland, the student would be obliged to follow the whole of, at least, a common core of subjects. It is difficult to resist the idea that British pupils who aspire to be teachers know that they can get by without a science or mathematics 'O' Level and simply do not work as hard if they happen to find the subject difficult.

The second major difference between Britain and the Continent is that, in Britain, the distinction between teaching higher and lower academic courses is very much blurred. British teachers are all on the same salary scale and, in principle, are qualified to teach any age group. There are differences in actual pay because of the greater number of promotion posts in secondary schools (a long standing grievance with the National Union of Teachers) and, in practice, it is unlikely that a primary or infant-trained teacher will move to a secondary school. However, the common pay structure and the common professional qualification has given the teaching profession in Britain a general status which is a rough average between that of the graduate sixth-form teacher and that of the infant-teacher who, in the past decade, has tended to be a woman, has tended to be young and has tended to have poor formal qualifications.

This regression towards the mean in status and pay has been avoided in most European countries by dividing the profession into different levels for different age groups with different qualifications, different pay and different status.

By this means, relatively high pay has been offered to upper secondary school teachers so that men and women of high academic quality have been attracted. The status of such teachers has been increased and, therefore, a high rate of applications has been maintained. Even at the lower levels, teaching has been more popular abroad than in Britain. In 1965, the percentage of those applying for primary school teacher training who were actually admitted to college was:

France	33 per cent
Sweden	42 per cent
Britain	90 per cent

(Source OECD)

It is clear, therefore, that the present generation of French and Swedish primary school teachers are a much more select group than those in Britain. The French have also maintained the prestige and the high academic standards of their best secondary school teachers through the competitive examination for the *agrégés* which have no parallel in Britain.

In 1972, for example, 18,000 candidates were competing in the examination for *agrégé* but only 2,200 were admitted. At the same time, 46,000 candidates were examined for the secondary school certificate (CAPES) of whom only 6,500 were admitted. France has a series of different teaching qualifications ranging from *instituteur* in primary schools, the CAPES in secondary schools, the *agrégé* in upper sixth forms and *professeur d'université* in higher education.

The fierce competition for the teaching of the most academic children makes a startling contrast with the position in Britain, where the total number of applicants for post-graduate teacher training in 1975 was only 16,000 of whom 5,400 withdrew. And all but a handful (1 per cent) were admitted to training places. Within that total there is a continuing shortage of modern language specialists. Only 766 were mathematicians so that, at the present rate, six years will be needed to train one new mathematics graduate for each secondary school in England and Wales.

The differentiation of teachers by academic level occurs in most other countries: in Holland, for example, there are three separate grades of teacher training certificate, entitling the holder to teach in pre-university schools, in the higher secondary schools or in the lower secondary and primary schools respectively. Plans are now afoot to supplement the initial training with compulsory in-service training for all teachers. These three tiers of qualification are similar to proposals for reform of teacher training in Germany promulgated by the *Bildungsrat*. The Swedish system is similar to our own, with a split between one year trained graduates and college training of two to three years for nursery, junior and middle level teachers. In Britain, the whole of initial training is in a period of unprecedented upheaval because of the declining birthrate and the consequent reduction in demand for teachers. Colleges are being closed or merged with polytechnics or diversifying to general courses. The detailed merits of this reorganization are beyond the scope of present study. The changes will not, however, solve the three related problems now faced by our system. They are:

Firstly how to attract a better field of applicants from which to select people of high calibre for secondary school academic teaching. Unless we are simply going to throw in the sponge in comprehensive schools, a great many more teachers of high academic calibre will be needed. This does not mean that they all have to be educated in traditional disciplines. As was argued earlier, the need for a greater vocational bias should, by no means, imply a lowering of intellectual standards. If anything, the reverse is the case. Only good would result if schools attracted a much higher proportion of sixth form teachers whose initial training was as engineers, accountants — even doctors and lawyers.

The second need is to recruit extra teachers in shortage subjects for which the nation has a long-term need. The present *laissez faire* attitude, coupled with exhortations, has no chance of succeeding.

Thirdly, minimum standards of entry into teacher training urgently need to be raised. Five GCE 'O' Levels is much too low a standard, even for students with a good personality who intend only to teach infants. All the evidence points to the importance of a good foundation in the infant and junior school. At this stage, the new methods being introduced from the colleges can quickly degenerate into playing about unless the teachers, themselves, apply standards of intellectual rigour. The educational standards of intending primary school teachers is lower than in France where the *instituteurs* must pass the *baccalauréat* before starting their two-year training in the *écoles normales.* Similarly, German elementary school teachers must pass the *Abitur* before starting their training. There is no doubt that, in some subjects, notably mathematics and languages, the German lower school teachers are much better qualified than their English equivalents. Those intending to teach in the *Gymnasium* have a truly formidable programme of five to ten years subject specialization after the *Abitur,* followed by two *Refendar* years of practical training in school.

The British should, therefore, ask whether the best way of improving recruitment to teaching would not be to make entry more *difficult* by raising the academic minima. An inisistence on two GCE 'A' Levels and five 'O' Levels including mathematics and preferably a science and a language might, even in the short-term, have a better effect on recruitment than is often assumed. It might merely mean that those wishing to become teachers would have to work harder at school in order to qualify. It is not sufficiently recognized that most youngsters are attracted to professions which are difficult to enter, partly for no other reason than that they are difficult. Teenagers want to accept a challenge and they assume that any profession which is difficult to get into is worthwhile. The present feeling amongst many recruits that teaching is a last-resort profession, depresses the morale of those who really do want to teach. The dramatically lowered demand for teachers will, in the next few years, provide an excellent opportunity to raise entry standards. Recruitment of good graduates could be similarly improved by introducing additional competition for higher pay and status. At present, extra pay is offered to graduates and good honours graduates but this, in itself, does not provide the incentive which is needed. The real need is to introduce extra rewards and status to those who are prepared to compete for them *after* they graduate. A competitive diploma carrying extra salary points and status would provide a method similar to the French *agrégé* exams. The number of awards could be related to the demand for particular subjects and would, therefore, provide a method of attracting mathematicians and linguists. However, there are good arguments for avoiding the narrow academicism shared by the *agrégé* and the German *Gymnasium* teachers. High intellectual quality should be assessed alongside personal qualities and the potential to be a good teacher. Those selecting for the top ranks of the Civil Service already make such efforts to choose the right people through simulated assignments and a range of sophisticated tests. A similar procedure for selecting potential high-fliers in the education service could do a great deal to enhance the prestige of the profession. And it might, incidentally, do a lot to shake the one year Diploma of Education for graduates out of its present torpor. Methods may differ, but at least as much care should be taken to recruit men and women of calibre into teaching as is spent on picking bureaucrats. If larger numbers of able people are to be attracted to teach in comprehensive school sixth forms, much more attention will be needed to ensure that they can do the kind of academic work which they want to do. The present tendency is to insist that graduate staff should teach throughout the school to classes of mixed ability eleven-year-olds as well as to highly specialized sixth form groups. Whatever the advantages of this development, there can be little doubt that at least some well qualified graduates either do not want, or are unsuited, to teach lower level classes. If such teachers cannot be accommodated, as they used to be in the sixth forms of grammar schools, they will not join the profession. In Holland and Germany, the traditional separation of academic children aged eleven and their teachers still persists. In France and Sweden, the two countries which have changed to comprehensive schooling, teachers with a specifically academic bent can still find a niche in the upper secondary schools, preparing for university entrance, while, in France the old *lycée* stream still exists in the upper three grades of the comprehensive. It is, without question, desirable that young children in comprehensive schools should be exposed to higher qualified staff and, indeed, many graduates prefer to teach younger age groups. However, the abrupt ending of university expansion will mean that, in the next decade, many graduates of a more donnish caste of mind will be potentially available for school teaching. If schools fail to attract them because of a dogmatic egalitarianism, the consequences for Britain will be extremely serious.

The recruitment of good teachers is, thus, closely linked with the consensus of values adopted by the profession which may, in the long term, have a profounder effect than government policy or the pay structure.

This consensus plays much of the part taken by explicit policy direction in other countries, because of the non-interference policy of the British government and the weakness and the internal divisions of local authorities. But, precisely because it is a consensus and not a policy, it is partly emotional, partly reasonable, partly incoherent and only partly what the country requires. The major task of policy-makers is now to influence this consensus and modify its operation, because few people would wish to scrap all the advantages of local autonomy and individual freedom and change to a thoroughgoing central system like that in France or Sweden. Huge central bureaucracies have many disadvantages of their own, as we are finding with the Health Service and some of the nationalized corporations.

The task, therefore, is to make the system more responsive to national policy, to the needs of industry and to the wishes of parents, without destroying scope for initiative and sensible experiment. To do this, means must be found to articulate at national level the educational aspirations and the needs of the community at large, as opposed to those emanating from the education system itself. The national committee, suggested earlier, should be the means for this. In addition, the inspectorate (HMI) should play a more vigorous part in identifying those schools or teachers acting in clear contradiction to national guidelines. Where necessary, governors, including the representatives of parents, should be informed of the discrepancies. This would provide, at least, some established check on whether a school was being steered into a tangent by extremists.

In addition, heads of all schools should be required to publish a statement of their general aims and philosophy as well as details of the curriculum and methods of teaching in their school. This statement should be distributed to parents, who should have a statutory opportunity of discussing any points they wish to raise on it, with the head and staff concerned. In cases of serious disagreement, parents should be entitled to the services of an arbitrator and, possibly, to a full inspection by HMIs. Thus, while teachers wield many of the powers which, in Europe, are exercised by the government, they should be under similar obligations to open up discussion of their purposes.

None of these suggestions would go as far in the direction of making teachers accountable to the community as is the common practice in Europe, though it must be said that the central bureaucracy in France, while exercising tight national control, does not give schools much scope for a flexible response to local wishes. A combination of our local authority traditions with a much more rigorous appraisal of national direction and effective checks by parents, could provide a hopeful compromise.

VIII. After Schooling – College, University and Work

Finally, after ten or twenty years of education, the teenager emerges, looking for a job. This is when employers find out whether the youngster has been adequately prepared and when the young applicant suddenly faces realities which may not have occurred to him during school and college days. Even those who emerge from the education system with no qualifications at all, may face similar anxieties to others with a doctors' or masters' degree — 'will there be a suitable job for me and will I need more training before I can do it properly?' Strangely, it may be the student with the PhD degree who has the greater worry, for his twenty years of continuous study may have done little to prepare him either practically or psychologically for many of the jobs open to him. The remoteness of much post-graduate work from the needs of industry was strongly criticised in the Parliamentary Expenditure Committee's report on Post-graduate Education (1974) which found that over 60 per cent of those gaining higher degrees in Britain were simply fed back into the education system. A further 13 per cent are doctors or dentists. In many other jobs, the long, demanding and expensive study counted for little. The committe said:

In the vast majority of occupations, a higher degree is of little or no value to the employer and may even be a handicap.

The reason is fairly obvious. The detailed research for a thesis is usually of little practical relevance outside a narrow field. The techniques used are different from the skills needed in the commercial or administrative worlds and may not even have much relevance to a company's research and development department. At the same time, the intensely personal style of work to which a PhD student becomes habituated, may unsuit him for the very different demands of earning a living.

If some of our cleverest youngsters are destined to be over-educated, very many school-leavers are seriously under-educated. In 1974, 300,000 British youngsters went into jobs where little or no further training was provided. Only 40 per cent of the school leavers entering employment could expect training (*Vocational Preparation for Young People,* Training Services Agency Discussion Paper, 1975).

Mr. John Cassells, the agency's chief executive, estimates that in Germany, 90 per cent of school leavers enter an apprenticeship with prescribed standards of training and compulsory day release for study at technical colleges. In a paper to the British Association for Commercial and Industrial Education (December 1975) he said:

> In Sweden, only ten per cent of youngsters fail to enter a vocational education course, the relevance of which to the world of work is often guaranteed by the fact that the syllabuses are provided by the employers' organizations. In France, there is something of the same story.

The consequence of Britain's improvident treatment of future manpower has been a continuous shortage of skilled workers since the War. As the Manpower Services Commission said in its first report for 1975-76:

> Practically every analysis of the labour market undertaken since 1945 has pointed out that, even when the general demand for labour has been relatively low, acute shortages of particular skills have persisted and that these have retarded economic growth.

It is worth noting that of the 600,000 French youngsters aged 16-19, who were looking for jobs in the summer of 1975, two-thirds had some kind of professional or technical training.

The answer of successive governments has been to try to increase training for specific skills by direct government agency or by incentives to industry. The government Training Boards were established with a levy system designed to encourage firms to train their recruits properly. This system led to an increase in the number of training places but has not been able to meet the need for imaginative training for the future needs of the country. This is because the training in large numbers of individual firms is variable and often poor while, at the same time, the bigger firms have been reluctant to train more youngsters than they foresee they will need themselves.

Then, in 1972, a national Training Opportunities Scheme was launched which aimed to provide a network of courses (mainly in technical colleges and Government Skill Centres) of up to a year in the skills needed by the economy. The target was to train 100,000 people per year, as soon as possible. The following year, the independent Training Services Agency was established and, in 1974, the Manpower Services Commission was formally established to try to promote a better match between the needs of industry and the training provided.

A lot of the past emphasis of government training schemes has been on the re-training of adults who have been thrown out of their jobs or who need to learn new skills. But, increasingly, attention is being turned on to the schools to ask what they are doing to fit teenagers for their first jobs, especially now that they keep them until age 16.

The result has been argument and discussion in industry about what schools should be doing. Some firms would like to see much closer links with the world of work, with more vocationally-orientated courses in the last two years. Others believe that the schools should concentrate on more effective teaching of the basic groundwork of reading, clear writing and mathematics. It is sometime argued that these aims may be incompatible for the least able youngsters. On the other hand, all experience shows that children who have fallen badly behind in learning the basic skills by the age of 13 or 14, are unlikely to make progress unless a new way can be found to fire their interest. And certainly, one way of doing this, would be to adapt the new 'integrated' methods of learning to courses which combine the three Rs and general education with the learning of skills needed in the employment market. In the short term, the only practicable way of achieving this in Britain would be through a much closer integration between the school and the technical college system, particularly in the last year. A number of experiments with 'linked courses' have recently been started but, as yet, they do not go nearly far enough to meet the national need. Most of the barriers to a flexible interchange are the administrative and conceptual ones rather than objections based on the real needs of teenagers. The administrative barriers, mentioned earlier, stem from the growth of different regulations and organization patterns governing technical colleges.

But they could be overcome if the will were there. More fundamental, is the conceptual fallacy that education and training are separate processes. People have become conditioned to thinking that adult life suddenly starts at 16 when pupils leave school. This idea is rapidly being broken down in Europe, although it still persists in many schools. In its report on *Education and Working Life,* (1975) the OECD comments:

> If young people cannot find jobs which satisfy them, they will continue to hang on in the educational system or drop out into the streets. If the separation of learning to be and learning to do continues, the practical will continue to be second best to the theoretical. Youth needs both. Yet the tendency, in the past, has been to assume that forces of change would gradually lead to a system of full time institutionalized education for all young people up to their late teens — a process which has gone furthest in the USA. This is a tendency whose inevitability and desirability we seriously question. Many young persons will want to start their working life at age 16 or so, as they do in the US, even when they are in full time education. The policy problem is how to provide a range of educational-work options for the whole teenage group. At the moment, no country has a coherent policy approach embracing the whole range of educational and training options for teenagers.
>
> An integrated system of curricular options should be more varied and more balanced than in most existing school systems. This requires co-operation between education authorities, employers and trade unions in order that the

options, especially vocational ones, can be formulated.
Pupils who combine school with work should have the
opportunity to combine courses of general education with
vocational ones, so that the option of access to higher
levels of education, at a later stage, is preserved and so that
they can adapt their vocational skills as economic structures
and technological change in future. Those who opt for
general courses of upper secondary education, should spend
part of their time getting practical experience relevant to
their academic work. This is not a proposal that employing
institutions should turn themselves into schools. On the
other hand, there can be little doubt that well-conceived
practical experience in the professions, industry, commerce,
administration or social service can have a profound
pedagogic value for young people, for the simple reason
that human learning, as distinct from animal learning, is a
dialogue between concept and practice.

A fundamental redefinition of the boundary between education and
training is particularly needed in Britain, not merely to introduce a
more practical element into schooling but to convince those running
training courses of the need for a continuing element of general
education.

In Europe, the importance of vocational training has generally been
better recognized than in Britain, although the training which produces
skilled craftsmen varies greatly from country to country. The main
difference is that, in some countries, like Germany, the emphasis has
been on company apprenticeship schemes with day release to technical
colleges, whereas France has, traditionally, relied upon government
sponsored off-the-job training. Both countries are, however, moving
towards a more compromise system. In Sweden, the majority of pupils
now stay on in the upper secondary school for institutionalized training,
usually lasting two years. However, efforts are being made to increase
the direct links with industry and particularly the extent to which people
alternate jobs with training, at least in their early careers. Continental
experience all points to the fact that neither college-based nor company-
based training schemes can, on its own, cope with the whole range of
training needs. College training can become too unrealistic and out of
touch with the precise needs of firms, whilst exclusively company-based
apprenticeships can be narrow in themselves and, inevitably, have little
regard for the long-term manpower needs of the economy. The answer
in Holland has been to start general technical training at a very early
age, in special technical schools which pupils join straight after their
primary school. An aspiring carpenter will, for example, start general
technical subjects at the age of twelve-plus, at the elementary technical
school. He takes a three year course, of which two-thirds of the first
year is spent in general education but a third of the time is spent on
woodworking and other general crafts. After the first 'orientation' year,
the pupil proceeds to more specialized courses where half the studies are
general and half are practical. In the third year, the carpenter will
specialize still further in, say, joinery or cabinet making. After school,
the pupil signs an apprenticeship agreement which includes theoretical

school training (one day a week, increased in August 1975 to two days a week). This system has, undoubtedly produced excellent craftsmen and has probably contributed to the hard working characteristics of the people. It is wrong to assume that the efficiency of their docks, ship repairers and other enterprises is the result merely of an in-built industriousness. After all, the British are historically an industrious nation too. The education and training of young people must mould, as well as reflect, the character of the adult workforce.

A similar observation can be made about the German efficiency in training young people which was given urgency after the last War, parallel to the enormous drive for industrial regeneration. The result was the development of the unique dual system which, at one time, was the envy of the world and continues to supply industry and commerce with highly trained personnel (*Germany,* OECD, 1972). This system provided between a day a week schooling in *Berufschule* or vocational school, coupled with a very thorough apprenticeship controlled by various industrial and commercial organizations and the Federal Ministry of Labour and Social Affairs. The factory floor training follows detailed schemes and is enforced by an examination system.

This system, though more comprehensive and more efficient than the British apprenticeship schemes, is now coming under similar criticism of narrowness and fragmentation. Efforts are therefore being made in several *Länder* (provinces) to introduce a pre-apprenticeship year of general technical training to prepare apprentices for a world in which particular skills can quickly become obsolete.

The Federal Government's pamphlet *Aktionsprogramme: Berufliche Bildung* (1970) which followed the Vocational Training Act *(Berufbildungsgesetz)* of 1969, explains the new perspective:

> The Federal Government has placed training policy at the head of internal reforms. Vocational training is an essential part of the total education system. For this reason, it has been declared to be part of the public responsibility on the same footing as general education. Vocational training must not be the stepchild of education policy and must not lag behind schools and high school reforms. For decades, it has been regarded as the self-administered task of industry. The Government appreciates the training achievements of industry. Today, however, the same vocational, political and pedagogic principles must apply to pupils, students and trainees alike.

The thoroughness of the German system of training can be estimated from the fact that, in 1972, there were 535 separately registered occupations for each of which a detailed training schedule has been drawn up for implementation by individual firms. (*Vocational Training in the EEC,* BACIE, 1972). The training profile for an Assistant Swimming Pool Superintendent, for example, runs to three closely printed pages covering safety, lifesaving and detailed schedules of the type of supervision and instruction which he is expected to master in the two-and-a-half year course. With hindsight, a strong case can be advanced that the money spent raising the school-leaving age to 16 in

Britain, could have been better spent introducing a modified version of the German dual system of training with, perhaps, greater emphasis on general education and a more substantial period in college.

The main problem about vocational training, which is exercising all European countries at present, is the potential conflict with the ideal of equal opportunity. Thus a Dutch youngster, who enters lower technical school (*LAVO*) at 12, has very little chance of ever climbing the educational ladder towards a higher technical qualification. If he opts to be a fitter, a fitter he will be, because the highly practical syllabus blocks off the chances of progression. Before condemning this inequality in the fashionable manner, we should observe that this kind of *Laufbahn* or lifetrack, as the Germans call it, is not evil for many youngsters who have no academic ambitions but wish to become masters of a craft or skill. On the other hand, there is a strong feeling that the end of primary schooling is too early a stage at which to set children on their different tracks. Consequently, the Netherlands Government has produced a comprehensive plan (*The Future Education Order,* 1975) which will defer specialized training until, after a general comprehensive middle school stage, from age 12 to 16. This is partly a response to the social inequalities inherent in all European education systems. In Holland, 60 per cent of the middle classes go to grammar schools compared with only 7 per cent of the working classes and the university population is overwhelmingly middle class.

In spite of egalitarian objections, early specialization is probably the most efficient method of producing good craftsmen as it is of promoting high academic standards. Indeed, with scarce resources and a high demand for skilled and qualified people, early specialization is inevitable. However, three factors are rapidly extending the period of general education in all countries. They are: the drive for greater equality of opportunity and social justice, coupled with a desire to increase the effort spent educating children as children rather than as future employees and, at the same time, the realization by educators that a wider base of general and technical knowledge is needed for an age in which new machinery will make retraining inevitable for many workers.

For this reason, a mainly general education in some sort of comprehensive school, up to the age of 16 is emerging (still only planned in Holland). Those countries which have gone comprehensive (Sweden and France) are increasingly realizing the danger of prolonging general education which is divorced from the realities of work.

At the same time, those who spend important years of teenage development cocooned in school, may, particularly if they are among the less successful pupils, become alienated from school, from society and from work.

Professor Torsten Husen chronicled some of the lost hopes and disillusionments which followed the extension of general education to all 16 year-olds in Sweden. (*The Learning Society* ibid):

When the 1962 education act increased the number of compulsory grades from seven to nine, the assumption was that pupils would receive an equivalent increment to their knowledge. Unfortunately, investigations made on an international basis seem to show that neither the assumption of high correlation nor the one of linearity comes anywhere close to being correct. Pupils who go to school every second day or every second term for seven years appear to learn just as much as those who are in attendance every day and every term during the period . . . The point is simply this: exposure to education beyond a certain level does not have the effect that we are inclined to ascribe to it. Here again, the law of diminishing returns applies. Analysis of Swedish data from the International Project for the Evaluation of Educational Achievement show that low motivated pupils even tend to lower their achievements in, for instance, science during the ninth year of compulsory schooling.

Professor Husen's warning should be particularly heeded by British policymakers, for the aim of giving a broadly similar general education to everyone up to the age of 16 has been more completely realized in Sweden than in any other West European country. The blind orthodoxy of believing that more education must be a good thing, irrespective of its type, and that abstract studies are superior to useful training, has already led Britain a long way down the same path. The Swedes are beginning to grapple with realities which, in Britain, are still largely confined to the murmuring of staffroom dissidents. In April, 1976, the Swedish Government proposed a series of reforms to schools, based on the four year commission on schooling and work (*skolans inre arbete*). A Bill before Parliament proposes a series of planning councils in every county and local authority area to improve contacts between school and working life. The councils would include representatives from schools, labour employment agencies, employers and trade unions. They are expected to help in giving tuition on employment and careers, including the present scheme under which senior pupils work full-time for a period during their final year, as part of their studies. The Bill suggests that trade unions should help schools and proposes improved forms of careers guidance.

Throughout Europe, it is becoming evident that conventional schooling is almost bound to fail with a certain group of older pupils who have lost interest in what is offered.

Yet some of these pupils are preparing to resume their studies later, after they have started work. The danger is that school teachers will engage in a frenetic search for 'innovations' to make the conventional programmes interesting; but they may only destroy the academic disciplines and fail to capture pupils who really want something else altogether. The only escape from this blind alley, must be a new conception of education and training as a unified process including school, college and work. Preparations for apprenticeship, or at least for the world of work, should start earlier in school life but general education should continue after the teenager has left school, by day release courses or apprenticeship schools, run in the larger companies.

Almost certainly, national policy will be needed which comprehends the major interests — schools, colleges, trade unions, employers and the training bodies. To forge a common policy out of all these different interests will be a formidable task, but a highly important one. To work out training policies for the 16 to 19 age group, as the present government is attempting, is not enough. Integration of training with school policies is also needed, so that careers guidance and vocational preparation can start effectively at the age of 13 or even younger.

If this is to be done, arguments about the need for more equality of opportunity must be taken seriously, for vocational training will simply fail to be accepted in schools if it is seen as a way of condemning school drop-outs to an inferior social position.

The answer must be to preserve and strengthen the alternative routes and 'second chances' which are, already, quite strongly built into our system — certainly much more than in France or Germany.

The success of the Open University has demonstrated, impressively, that many people are prepared to work extraordinarily hard, in their own time, to gain extra qualifications and that early failure in the education system may not be a barrier to later success. The principle of a second chance needs to be extended to teenagers and young adults who, having trained for a specific vocation, discover an interest and ability for further general study. The technical colleges already do a good job to help them, but the lack of day release opportunities for many youngeters is often a barrier to further study. Sweden, the Netherlands and Germany all have better arrangements for day release than we do, with systems of part time education for everybody up to the age of 18. In France, an attempt to promote further training amongst the work-force was made in 1972 when a new law obliged firms to spend up to 2 per cent of their wage bill on training and give every employee the right to training.

The system is analagous to the levies imposed by the Industrial Training Boards in Britain but the main difference is that it aims to improve the training of the established work force rather than that of new entrants. The system has worked reasonably well but it is open to abuse. Trade unions have complained that the money is sometimes used for glorified holidays for executives on 'study courses' abroad, rather than for training workers. Nevertheless, the scheme shows a seriousness of purpose about adult or continuing education which is lacking in Britain.

One of the most important benefits in lowering the fences between education, training and working life, should be to promote greater interchange between school and college teachers and people in industry, commerce and the professions. Thus, more teachers should go into industry, not merely for sherry with the personnel manager, but to take part in the practical training of adult and apprentice workers. Similarly, schools should become more open to people from industry and the professions who may be able to contribute to pupils' wider educational

111

studies as well as to their more specific vocational needs. Such interchange is vital to help modify the prejudice amongst teachers against the world of work and the feeling amongst some people in schools that their main task is to educate pupils for increasing leisure. At the same time, industrialists need to appreciate their responsibility for continuing the opportunities for general and personal education. Without a substantial shift of attitude in both directions there can be little hope that organizational changes will, by themselves, bring much improvement. On the other hand, those who pin their hopes, merely on better co-operation and understanding, are naïvely optimistic. A strong government lead would be welcomed by many teachers and employers.

University and College

Any discussion of the relationship between the worlds of work and education must take account of the responsiveness of higher education to society. Certainly, there is a widespread feeling that the universities' concentration on esoteric academic studies has given many students an inappropriate preparation for the lives they will later lead. But the claims of practical education have to be balanced against the universities' assertion that their real purpose is the pursuit of knowledge; or alternatively, that the training of students' minds and habits of thought is much more important than the subject area in which it is achieved. However, the traditional argument that the study of Greek can help develop the mental power needed in, say, a top civil servant or manager, can be inverted. It may simply be that someone who is clever enough to shine at Greek is clever enough to run a department. The study of a difficult practical subject at a university, might have made him an even better manager. This argument was of little importance when only an elite of 2 or 3 per cent went to university. But in an age of mass higher education, the question is much more urgent. In 1973-74, the proportion of school leavers in England and Wales, going on to degree courses had risen to 6.5 per cent, while a further 2.3 per cent started training to be teachers. Overall, 20 per cent of the age group went on to some form of further study after school. (DES 1975).

Although university expansion is now declining due to lack of money, there can be little doubt that the long term demand in Britain will follow that of all other advanced industrial nations for a continuing increase in the provision of higher education. The establishment of the polytechnics, following the 1966 White Paper, *A Plan for Polytechnics and other Colleges* (CMND 3006) was a recognition of the need to concentrate the expansion into institutions which would tend to develop students' practical competence rather than the pursuit of pure learning. A clear statement of their role was made by the late Mr. Anthony Crosland in his speech at Woolwich in April 1965. In his address to a conference on their future in June, 1972, Mr. Crosland severely criticized some of the polytechnics for trying to put on the academic mantles of universities and he said that few were showing signs of filling the function for which they were created.

The difficulty is that, in spite of a strong consensus emerging amongst politicians and administrators about the need for more practically orientated degrees and close links with the community in polytechnics, no effective means has been created for articulating a national policy for the whole of higher education or for enforcing it at local level.

The Department of Education's and the Secretary of State's powers over higher education policy are extremely limited — as indeed they are over most other sorts of education.

Universities jealously guard their independence and, even though the bulk of their money comes from the public purse, they are cushioned from public control by the University Grants Committee. Polytechnics, on the other hand, are financed by an absurd system of pooling, which is a national fund created from local authority finances, part of which come from the national government in the first place. This has led to a range of fiscal absurdities and great difficulty in exerting financial discipline over institutions; for controlling authorities are, in effect, spending other people's money. More important, the fragmentation of control in the local authority sector and the gulf which separates it from universities, has made the development of public policy extremely difficult.

To some extent, the system is self-regulating, because all institutions are competing for students. The polytechnics, particularly, have been under pressure to provide courses which will, at the same time, attract students and lead to a career at the end of the course. The provision of courses has been further regulated by the need to secure approval from the Council for National Academic Awards for all new degrees, by the veto which the Department of Education and Science can exercise over courses which do not attract enough applicants and by central control over new capital projects. However, a new national organization is now needed to administer the higher education sector as a whole. For this pupose, a Higher Education Grants Committee was proposed by the Education and Arts Sub-Committee of Parliamentary Expenditure Committee (1972). But the proposal was rejected on the grounds that a body administering some 550 institutions, if further education were included, would be too cumbersome. Undoubtedly, there are difficulties, but they are difficulties which have been overcome in other European countries where universities and colleges are controlled centrally or, in the case of Germany, regionally.

The importance of central planning was convincingly argued by the Carnegie Commission, which produced 22 reports on higher education in the USA. It said, in 1971:

In its broadest sense, statewide planning must first be concerned with sets of goals: the economic and the social goals of the state, the goals of the education system and its institutions, the goals of individuals within the system and the interaction among these sets of goals.

In Continental Europe, the importance of central planning for higher education has been thoroughly recognized. In France, a complete re-organization of the university system took place in 1968 through the Orientation Law. Germany and the Netherlands have also introduced laws governing the universities in 1970, and all three countries have made attempts, in the last few years, to draw up comprehensive plans for the future of higher education. The most spectacular planning attempt was made by the Swedish U 68 Commission on Higher Education (1973) which attempted to relate higher studies fairly closely to forecasts of future manpower needs and to produce a detailed plan which would relate the different institutions throughout the country. The U 68 Commission calculated the requirements for 12 occupational groups and, on the basis of these figures, suggested the number of places which should be made available in different sectors of higher education. The Commission admitted that great caution is needed in making manpower predictions and, frequently stressed the high margins of possible error. However, the Swedes believe, unlike the British, that a reasonable estimate is better than none at all. In Sweden, as in other European countries, university and college staffs are civil servants and, consequently they have never had the autonomy which their opposite numbers in Britain enjoy. A greater distinction is made between the academic freedom required for research and the freedom to design courses, which is clearly circumscribed. The U 68 report, for example, said that each higher education institution should have a planning committee for each occupational sector, only a third of whose members should be teaching staff, a third should be students and a third from occupational life. These committees should have powers to establish syllabuses, to review the content, organization and capacity of courses and to draft guidelines for educational and vocational guidance.

The public interest in higher education should be further strengthened, U 68 said, by the creation of area boards on which six out of the ten members should represent public interests.

Clearly, a good case can be made against too much bureaucratic control of higher education. It can be repressive and unimaginative and result in very dull courses, as has happened in France. Alternatively, lay representatives on course committees may be narrow and philistine in their approach. A manpower planning approach is also open to objections not merely that the planners will get their figures wrong, but that the students will be dragooned into courses which they do not want to study which may not, after all, lead to a job and which will restrict their opportunities of finding alternative employment.

However, these difficulties should not blind us to the need for a more rational approach to higher education planning and, particularly, to increasing the vocational content of courses for those students who want them. All the current evidence points to the fact that very many students prefer to study for degrees which are directly related to a profession.

The latest figures from the Universities Central Council on

Admissions, for example, show that the most popular courses are law, medicine, veterinary science and other vocational subjects with professional status. Engineering is unpopular but this can be attributed, very largely, to poor maths teaching rather than an antipathy to vocational studies.

Many of the less popular subjects are those with no obvious professional outlet. It seems clear that, to attract a better flow of able graduates into industry, two conditions are necessary. First, the occupations themselves must be seen to carry high prestige and to be intrinsically interesting. Industry will have to make more efforts to present its career opportunities to students. Secondly, degree courses need to be orientated more closely to these jobs. Even a small shift in this direction could have a considerable moral effect throughout the higher education institutions.

Before this can happen, the country needs to do a lot of thinking aloud about the system as a whole. The enormous increases in state finance have inevitably brought increases in state control, but controls have not been organized by any consistent vision. A national commission is needed to start this and to promote a much sharper conception of the differences between the purely institutional views of education and the wider needs of the community.

IX. Summary and Conclusion

The evidence points, from two different directions, to the same conclusion: that schools are not giving nearly enough attention to the values and skills which children will need in their future working lives and that academic standards are, in some subjects, much lower than they should be. On the one hand, the evidence that we need more emphasis on rigour, hard work and tighter standards comes from parents and employers and a growing band of educationists in Britain. The same conclusion is suggested by comparison with current education practice in the major industrial countries of Europe.

In most of these countries, the total volume of education (including nursery schooling and vocational training) has now outstripped that in Britain. In Germany, for example, all children stay in part time education up to the age of 18 while the great majority also get full time apprenticeship training to the same age. In Sweden, also, most children stay in the upper secondary schools for vocational or academic courses up to age 18.

In terms of quality, the output of British education is much patchier than elsewhere because we are unique in not imposing minimum standards or, at least, an outline curriculum on schools. Because of this slacker control, it seems probable, although hard data is scarce, that competence in the basic learned skills is generally higher on the continent than in Britain. Our ability to equip 18 year-olds with the minimum academic requirement for university has, for some time, been inferior to that in Sweden or France and is now being rapidly outstripped by Germany. Even though the academic standard of individual GCE 'A' Level subjects may be higher than the equivalent abroad, the range of subjects required is considerably narrower. The present stagnation in the 'A' Level success rate is, therefore, disturbing when equivalent figures on the Continent are showing a steep upward trend. The fall in the pass rate in individual subjects, including maths and languages, is particularly distressing.

Furthermore, the inadequacy of technical training and vocational education in Britain is now generally recognized. Provision is strikingly inferior to that in Sweden, Germany or Holland — countries which have taken this aspect of education more seriously than we have for many years. The integration of technical and academic education in the Swedish upper secondary schools, should be an important example to us.

So should the dual apprentice training in Germany, provided by individual companies, but regulated nationally. At the same time, we need to consider the desirability of introducing more practical subjects to pupils below the age of 16, as the Dutch have done for years. However, the Dutch system of highly specialized vocational schools would be neither practicable nor desirable in this country. The solution should be a more integrated concept of general secondary education in which the vocational, the liberal and the personal elements were combined.

These criticisms highlight the almost total absence of control over what goes on in British schools and the loose attitude to standards of all but the abler pupils who take GCE. The degree to which the state and local authorities have shuffled off responsibility is unique in Europe. The extensive freedom of teachers, coupled with new methods of teaching, comprehensive re-organization and the political pressure for equality, have all taken place at the expense of preparing pupils for jobs. This trend has been further accentuated by the tendency, in an age of increasing prosperity, to see education more as a consumption of wealth than as an essential process in its generation.

Thus, in many teachers' minds, schooling has become identified with the idea of improving pupils' taste, imagination and powers of thinking rather than equipping them with useful skills and knowledge or making them disciplined members of society. They have aimed to extend the cultural and intellectual development previously reserved for any elite, to a much wider public.

These aims are laudable but they have been pursued too much at the expense of the practical demands of society. And the teaching profession has been too slow to develop subjects like navigation, horticulture and business economics which could provide an intellectual challenge to a wide range of pupils as well as being specifically useful to a minority. Curricula have also not combined enough practical subjects with those more academic or cultural, like literature, history and social science. If the haphazard development of school courses is allowed to continue without the discipline of a national policy, the gulf between school and working life is likely to increase. On the other hand, a retreat to narrow vocational training would, besides being unpopular, fail to meet the changing needs of technology which demands flexible rather than specific skills from the work force. A new integrated approach to academic and practical learning for the clever, as well as the duller pupils, should therefore be given a high priority. It is change which would be of more fundamental importance to children's education than the argument about physical integration into comprehensive schools.

Meanwhile, the re-organization of local government left the local education authorities without any effective national leadership. Mainly because of the pressure from the Labour Party, two-third of the new authorities refused to join the Association of Education Committees, which traditionally represented their interests. The authorities, therefore, have had three bodies speaking for them — the Association of Municipal Authorities, the County Councils' Association and the AEC — with the Council of Local Education Authorities (CLEA) a weak and ineffective sibling of the two former bodies. With such confusion of spokesmen, it is small wonder that consideration of policy was short term and fragmentary. On the Continent, education planning is accepted as part of the central government's responsibility but, in Britain, the division of control has meant that little concerted thought has been given to the kind of system which will be needed in future decades and, still less about how to achieve it. The Department of Education and Science takes a passive role of reacting to events and political pressures while, at the same time, trying to anticipate future trends. The immense power vested in the central administration in France and Sweden has made forward planning easier and has led to the development of truly national systems. It is often said that the big bureaucracies of a central system breed a narrow traditionalism. This used to be true in France but the speed of reforms, including the development of comprehensive schooling, belie this assumption.

Between the extremes of France, with only one education authority, and Britain which has 125, the German system of autonomous provinces might seem to be the ideal compromise. The provinces (or *Länder*) are big enough to be efficient but provide enough decentralization to prevent a wholesale sweep by an ideologically-minded central government. The effect has been to produce first, a sluggish and now a cautious approach to reform. On comprehensive education, for example, the Christian Democratic Union (CDU) have opposed all but a very gradual change. Even the socialist Social Democratic Party (SDP) is now proceeding extremely cautiously. The 160 experimental comprehensives only take pupils up to the age of 16 so that, even where they exist, the brighter pupils have a chance to transfer to a *Gymnasium* (grammar school).

The spirit of caution amongst German politicians of the Left, undoubtedly reflects the diffusion of power within the education service as well as the fact that the Germans have, to some extent, defused protests against 11-plus selection (10-plus in Germany) by giving greater freedom to make choices of secondary school.

The devolution of power in Germany has, then, brought a degree of stability which was a disadvantage during the 1950s and early 1960s when provision of school and college education fell behind that in most European countries. But the stability may now prove an advantage when the pace of educational change in Europe is out-stripping the resources and skills needed to make the reforms effective.

However, this devolution has increasing disadvantages which run parallel to some of the long-term problems facing Britain. Firstly, the financing of education must, inevitably, become more and more a matter for public national policy as schools and colleges consume an increasing share of the nation's wealth. Recently, the Layfield Committee on British local authority finance underlined the unsatisfactory consequences of allowing authorities to spend money — a large proportion of which they do not have the responsibility of raising. This is why, in Germany, the central government has taken an increasing interest in education, particularly in higher education and why, in Britain, the Department of Education and Science has assumed powers of veto over almost all educational spending.

The second, and possibly more important reason for the developing interest of central government is that the regional divisions in European countries are rapidly breaking up. People change jobs, whole families move house — perhaps two or three times — whilst children are growing up. Faster travel, increased car ownership, television and newspapers all contribute to the break-up of regional cultures. The German public has demanded a full equivalence of certificates and school organization so that families can move with the minimum of disturbance to their children. This demand for a regional equality has been the main fulcrum through which the Federal Education Ministry has exerted leverage on the *Länder* governments. Even school curricula the traditional responsibility of the *Länder,* are now being brought closely into line by national negotiations.

In some ways, the British government has wielded stronger powers to promote uniformity but this had been mainly restricted to the resources of staff and buildings. Thus, the quota system has ensured a rough equality of school staffing throughout the country, whilst building allocations and the conditions imposed on local authorities applying for loan sanction, have done the same for bricks and mortar.

A theme of this study has been the striking contrast between Britain and Europe in the lack of central direction over the organization and curriculum of schools. The famous 1944 Education Act did try to impose a uniform structure with, for example, a definition of only two types of allowable schools — primary and secondary. After 1964, the development of middle schools was allowed and the result has been a veritable chaos of change-over dates. Children can now be found changing to a different type of school at age 8, 9, 11, 12, 13, 14 and 16 in different parts of the country and this list leaves out the important change at age 7 from infant to junior school. Not all children will make these changes, of course, but the effect on a child whose parents happen to make a few unlucky moves may be highly disturbing especially as the curriculum in a middle school may be significantly different from that in a nearby secondary school. Moreover, the lack of central or local control over the school curriculum may mean that a child who moves school may have to cope with radically different styles of teaching as well as a changed content in his lessons.

The chaos which is now being organized is the consequence of forcing the pace towards a comprehensive school system whilst allowing all 125 local authorities to develop their own pet schemes. The argument has been that local people know the best scheme to fit local geography. But, in practice, educational theory has been at least as powerful a determinant of local comprehensive schemes as councillors' perceptions of the distinct needs of their areas. Meanwhile, the national politicians, embroiled in the question of whether to have a comprehensive system at all, have forgotten the far more difficult and more important question of how it is to be done.

The Labour Party has been so dazzled by a naïve vision of equality that it has not bothered to think out the consequences. And the Conservative Party has been so diverted by the slovenliness of the Labour Party that it has failed to produce any concerted alternative. As a result, the buck has been passed to local authorities. Ministers have retreated to their powers of veto under the 1944 Act and their pronouncements on national policy have been restricted to general sentiments delivered to the annual conferences of teachers.

The devolution of planning to local authorities has been matched, in Britain, by a further devolution of control over curriculum to individual schools. This has happened by a slow drift of responsibilities rather than by any act of public policy and is difficult to justify, however excellent the individual results may claim to be. In his lucid report on the collapse of the William Tyndale School, London, Mr. Robert Auld, Q.C. underlined the fact that local authorities cannot escape their legal responsibility for what goes on in schools, however much they choose to delegate. Immediately after the publication of his report, Sir Ashley Bramall, the leader of the authority, admitted that they had forgotten to exercise some of the powers vested in them and he put in hand, an immediate review of the local inspectorate to tighten up control over schools and to review the function of school managers, governors, and the teachers themselves. The need for a redefinition of these relationships led to the setting up of the Taylor Committee into school governors and managers.

It is not too cynical to observe that the setting up of the committee may have been a way for the Government to shuffle off a very obvious problem which it did not have resolution enough to tackle. It is further worth observing that few, if any, changes in the law would be needed by a Government determined to exert tighter supervision over the education system. Ministers already have considerable powers through building allocations and the operation of Section 13 procedures (Section 13 of the 1944 Education Act gives the Minister right of veto, after time for public objections, over every proposal by a local authority to make significant alterations in the character of a school).

This section already gives the government great powers over the organization of education in each locality. What has been lacking is a detailed policy which would give them the greatest incentive to co-operate in a uniform national pattern.

On curricular matters, ministers have simply chosen to abandon the influence which they formerly exercised and which they could, in theory, resume at any time they wished. As Dr. Karl Roloffs, head of planning at the German Federal Ministry of Education, remarked:

If I had the HMIs, I would control the system.

The HMIs used to issue curricular guidelines which included an indication of standards which were expected of schools. But they no longer do so. The inspectorate ceded this task to the Schools Council in the optimistic hope that serving teachers would identify the needs of the schools. But, for reasons already summarized, the Council failed, even with a multi-million pound budget to formulate, let alone disseminate, clear and generally accepted aims for our schools. In default of such work, the present Government has been forced to set up an Assessment and Performance Unit within the Department of Education to try to work out an acceptable basis for measuring standards, particularly in primary schools.

The pace of this work is, however, disappointingly slow and there is a danger that the simple practical issue of trying to ensure that children are learning the basic skills effectively may be obscured in a Utopian search for perfect tests. Researchers now want to measure whole batteries of related skills centering round old-fashioned concepts of reading, writing and arithmetic. However desirable improved tests may be, the search for them may prove to be a political red herring.

An over-sophisticated test may provide too many loopholes for the lazy, the inefficient or the sentimental teacher. And the instruments needed by skilled researchers may be inadequate for ensuring that children make progress and for reassuring parents. Even as an instrument for national sampling, tests which measure a dozen or more related skills will provide material for endless dispute. If, for example, the results seem to show a decline in the standard of arithmetic, it will always be open for teachers to point out some other ability, like spatial relationships, where standards may have improved. We will then merely have quantified the confusion which already exists between standards and objectives. How can the teachers possibly produce consistent standards if they are not given clear guidance about what they are to produce them in?

This confusion has no parallel in any other European country, where objectives, as well as the standards, are more or less clearly defined as public policy. The trend in France, Germany, Holland and Sweden is to give teachers greater freedom over matters of instruction but these countries have not chosen to emulate the tombola of objectives which our free enterprise teachers provide.

The diversity of aims and methods would not matter if the results had produced a general confidence amongst the public. Such confidence did exist during the early 1960s and, in some cases, it reached an almost Panglossian euphoria. It has now been replaced by acute anxieties described in the introduction of this study and elsewhere. Public concern about the effect of progressive teaching was recently given the most striking confirmation by the research findings of Dr. Neville Bennett of Lancaster University (chapter 3). This report marks a turn of the tide which was running in the 1960s when the Plowden Report (Children and their Primary Schools, 1967) sang the virtues of progressive teaching without giving nearly enough attention to its dangers.

The Plowden report and the general optimism which pervaded it was the product of a consensus between educationists in both parties, the main teachers' unions and the press correspondents around a somewhat left of centre progressive ideal. Cash was flowing, class sizes were steadily falling and higher education was starting its biggest boom in history. Above all, the intellectuals were advancing a cornucopia of new ideas and techniques for improving school teaching.

They included: language laboratories, new 'audio visual' techniques for teaching French in primary schools, the 'learn as you play' ideas for teaching maths and other subjects in primary schools, the project method, the integrated day, vertical grouping (putting two or three primary school age groups together), open plan classrooms — all these innovations had their passionate advocates.

In secondary schools, there was the new maths, Nuffield Science, a plethora of new integrated courses, a new exam (the CSE) for less able children; a new involvement by teachers in the planning of courses and the running of exams — hailed as the loosening of the straight-jacket; the disappearance of the much-disliked 11-plus and the entry of comprehensive schools under the slogan 'grammar schools for all'. And to crown it all, there was the raising of the school leaving age to 16, universally supported as a milestone in the history of compulsory education.

The intractable problem of children in the slums was to be tackled by a bipartisan policy to provide 'positive discrimination' and to break the 'cycle of deprivation'. And to underpin all these efforts was the re-improvement of the education of teachers. The new three year courses for teachers heralded the all-graduate profession.

It is hardly surprising that many distinguished educationists and commentators viewed these new horizons, like stout Cortez, with wild surmise of wonder and optimism. Most of those hopes have now crumbled. The problems have proved more intractable than was expected, the solutions more limited and the capacities of teachers sometimes inadequate to meet the new demands made upon them. It would be wrong, however, to lurch from over-optimism to excessive despair. The important lesson to be relearned is that educational progress is inevitably slow. Bright ideas and new technology cannot outrun the abilities of teachers. We have discovered that improved methods, badly applied, are often worse than the traditional techniques they replaced.

We should not forget that the major reforms in Sweden were accompanied by a much greater research effort and, more important, a huge increase in spending. Even under such favourable conditions, the results have not been satisfactory. In Germany and France, reforms have been more gradual than in Britain and, because of the greater central control over the systems, they have been preceded by periods of experimentation and evaluation. In Britain, changes need to be given much more careful study before they become widespread, while standards need to be closely monitored. We can no longer accept the bland assumption that the majority of teachers will adapt to do extra work. We should also be wary of the belief that extra difficulties can be overcome by better training and retraining of teachers. All the evidence so far is that the retraining of teachers has been unpopular and not very effective.

A period of consolidation and review is needed. This could be best promoted by central initiative from the Department of Education and Science, which should:

1.   Draw up guidelines for the standards expected in different ability ranges from all children in the age range seven to 13. This would follow the practice of our Continental neighbours.
2.   Consider the advantages of formal national tests for all children (not just samples as proposed by the present Government) at ages 7, 10 and 14. This would follow the recent practice in Sweden and would be a substitute for the yearly grades which children in France and Germany must pass.
3.   Issue detailed curricular guidelines in different subjects, including suggestions for a common core of studies for the majority of children.
4.   Request or require local authorities to publish their own curricular guidelines if they wished to vary from the national pattern.
5.   Ensure that all schools publish full details of any deviations they were making from the local authority curriculum.
6.   Publish detailed and frequent guidance to teachers in the HMIs views of new teaching methods and good practice.
7.   Issue national guidelines on homework.
8.   Encourage all schools to establish parent-teacher associations.

These eight measures would not significantly alter the balance of control of our education system because local authorities would still be in charge of their schools to whom they would be able to delegate as much responsibility for curriculum and methods as they chose. The measures would, however, explain to the public how great was the degree of delegation in each area and give parents a clear idea of the variations between the policies of the different schools. The proposal for monitoring children's standards would give a long-overdue estimate of the success of different school policies as well as providing an early warning about weak schools, poor teachers or groups of children in particular difficulties.

These eight measures would bring our education service roughly into line with the common practice in Europe without unduly damaging the much-prized freedom of schools to exercise their own initiative and enterprise.

The measures would, undoubtedly, provoke opposition from the organized teachers' unions but they would not essentially be more than an administrative effort to tighten up the present system, to make present practices explicit and to make them more efficient.

In addition, we need to give national thought to the long-term aims of the education service and to the policy implications of curriculum changes which are taking place or which may be needed in the future. Some of these issues involve fundamental political questions about the nature and ambitions of present day society. It is important that they should be carefully formulated even if they cannot all be resolved. In all other European countries, these questions are recognized to be political in the widest sense and they are the subject of decisions by governments in consultation with outside bodies. In Britain, no body exists for the public discussion of these questions of the overall balance and aims of schooling — except the Schools Council, which cannot properly consider the wider national context. The Schools Council should, therefore, be phased out in favour of a new advisory council with a more general brief to formulate advice to the minister on educational issues. Teachers should have a significant but minority voice on the new council which should represent as wide a spectrum of public interests as possible, including the political parties and local authorities.

The council should be able to stand back from the educational scene to assess the long-term implications of policies or lack of them, and particularly to consider their effects on economic progress. It should undertake similar planning exercises to those of the Swedish Board of Education and it should take steps to ensure that the broad projections of the Manpower Services Commission are, at least, taken into account in the planning of school curricula and educational developments. The other main topics which should lie before the Advisory Committee and, of course, the Department of Education are:

1. A major re-think about the proper balance between theoretical studies and the practical or vocational. It should make suggestions for introducing cleverer pupils to vocational options in the sixth forms or even earlier. The distinction between school work and apprenticeship training should be much less sharp than at present. The committee should advise on ways of integrating the two phases in a teenager's life and to increase part time education after school leaving.

2. Much closer integration in the upper secondary schools and the technical colleges is needed. The committee should review experiments in linked courses and advise on possible changes of the law to allow pupils to spend all, or part, of their last two years of compulsory schooling in college.

3. A major review of the advantages of different forms of comprehensive schools should be undertaken, with special attention to

methods of internal selection for different lines of study. The desirability of following Continental practice of separating upper secondary schooling (after age 16) into a separate sector, should be carefully considered as a way of improving sixth form standards, making better use of scarce specialist teachers and attracting new teachers of high academic calibre. Efforts should be made to reduce to a minimum the diversity of change-over ages for pupils in different authorities. A slowing down of the pace of change to comprehensive schooling is needed until these problems have been more carefully thought out.

4. The desirability of insisting on a common core of studies for all resonably able children should be urgently considered. An overall certificate to encourage a wide spread of GCE 'O' Level subjects should be considered, especially as this is the usual in Europe. At Advanced Level, the policy implications of widening the spread of subjects to three minor and two specialist subjects should be considered independently of the Schools Council's present feasability studies. The proposals for a Certificate of Extended Education for less able 17 year-olds and a common exam for all 16 year-olds should be shelved until the Council and the Government have thoroughly explored the vocational needs of the curriculum and the feasibility of integrating technical colleges (1 & 2 above).

5. Better methods of making teachers accountable to the parents they serve need to be explored. Encouragement of parent-teacher associations may need to be supplemented with statutory provisions to

    a) establish parents' councils and

    b) give parents the right of appeal where they are dissatisfied with a school's curriculum and cannot obtain a suitable transfer.

Noisy parents must not be allowed to obstruct schools — a filtering process would, therefore, be needed, possibly in the form of an independent appeals council composed equally of teachers and laymen. More parent governors would be an alternative but probably less effective method for safeguarding parents' interests.

6. The establishment of a national school leaving certificate, similar to the European pattern should be considered. It would give details of behaviour, attendance and non-academic achievements, as well as exam results. It should be available to future employers and could act as a powerful incentive for good behaviour in school.

The Government also need to consider two further measures which would probably be outside the scope of a newly constituted advisory committee. They are:

1. An immediate raising of the standard of entry to the teaching profession. A minimum of two 'A' Levels and five 'O' Levels including maths and either a science or a language, should be the immediate goal. In the longer run, three 'A' Levels should not be considered unrealistic,

or preferably two specialist 'F' Levels and two or three subsidiary 'N' Levels, under the revised system. These stipulations would not by any means be too high compared with the requirements of Continental countries.

2. The establishment of a Higher Education Commission, to oversee all institutions offering degree level courses. It should incorporate the University Grants Committee, which could continue to exist under its main umbrella. The functions of the Commission should be to administer, finance and co-ordinate higher education policy as a whole. It should consider, in general terms, the balance of available courses in relation to expected national needs. It might need reserve powers to compel institutions to change the balance of the courses they offered but, initially, persuasion and financial pressure should be used. Detailed suggestions for making universities and polytechnics more economical will, almost certainly, have to be made but this vast topic is outside the scope of this study.

The idea of a national council to advise the Education Secretary is hardly novel for, under the 1944 Education Act, the Secretary of State is required to have a Central Advisory Council. This council was active until 1966, when it was disbanded after finishing work on the Plowden Report on Primary Schools.

It was allowed to die for several reasons. The first was a dislike of the slow pace with which it produced long and cumbersome reports. Second the reports tended to study only one aspect of the service and, therefore, to become blinkered or to lapse into special pleading. This meant that they, inevitably, demanded extra money for improvements which the Government could not necessarily afford. Thirdly, the Plowden Report, in spite of its valuable descriptions of primary schooling, gave a too uncritical endorsement to the progressive consensus. It was regarded as an encyclical by many teachers who were encouraged to change their teaching methods faster than was efficient. Lengthy reports like Lady Plowden's are apt to 'discover' a new philosophy which turns out later to have been no more than part of the endless cycle of fashions which pervade the education service.

So, after the Plowden Report, ministers preferred to set up *ad hoc* enquiries with a limited brief: Sir Lionel Russell on adult education; Sir Alan (now Lord) Bullock on reading standards; Lord James on teacher training and now, Tom Taylor on school management. Of these, the James Report, was the only one to be lucid, straightforward and brief (the Taylor committee is still sitting). Certainly, none of them has been able to give the coherent long-term thought to the wider aims of the education service.

There are, therefore, two choices. One is to leave the Central Advisory Council in its grave and set up a completely new body. However, this hardly seems necessary when the law already prescribes consultations which, in the words of Lord Butler in 1944, were intended 'by reviewing the position continually, to consider the whole question of what may be taught to children'.

To avoid pitfalls of the past, the Central Advisory Council would have to maintain closer links with the Secretary of State while, at the same time, including a substantial number of people from outside the education industry. It must be prevented from running up the blind alleys of over-specialized topics and it should eschew detailed research which is much better left to outside bodies.

Under these conditions, the Advisory Council could undertake the long-term review which is needed. But, ultimately, it is the Secretary of State who matters. The necessary changes in the balance of power and the redefinition of objectives can only be brought about by a Secretary of State with the political will and determination to overcome inertia and inevitable opposition from teachers' unions.

The suggestions for effecting these changes can be summarized as follows:

1. A redefinition by the Government of the chain of authority in the service aimed to
   a) Illuminate present obscurities.
   b) Ensure that those at present vested with duties and authority discharge them properly.
   c) Ensure that devolution of power to individual schools and to teachers generally, happens by explicit intention, rather than by default.

2. Administrative action to promote a more uniform curriculum and much closer monitoring of standards as outlined in the eight points above.

3. A rebirth of the Central Advisory Council, to advise ministers on the long-term planning of education and to identify the decisions on school curricula which should depend upon national policy. Five of the urgent issues for consideration are listed above.

These proposals represent a compromise between allowing the present highly fragmented service to continue its drift and a move to the much more centralized controls of Continental countries. The aim should be to preserve the desirable freedom of teachers and local authorities but to require them to be exercised in a tighter framework. Teachers need to be made more directly accountable to parents locally and to the express will of the public as a whole. The liberal humanistic assumptions which now pervade the education service need to be challenged sharply by the more practical requirements of industry and commerce and of the majority of parents. That does not mean that the argument for practical studies should always win, nor that we should revert to the utilitarianism of Samuel Smiles. For industrialists and parents may often be wrong. However, teachers must equally recognize that they can be mistaken, not merely as individuals but in the major assumptions which pervade their profession. In the last ten years, teachers have persuaded the public that they have the right to determine what and how pupils are taught with almost no interference from anybody else. This proposition is not accepted in any other European country and it used not to be accepted in Britain.